Paul and Jesus

The True Story

David Wenham

WILLIAM B. EERDMANS PUBLISHING COMPANY
GRAND RAPIDS, MICHIGAN / CAMBRIDGE U.K.

Originally published 2002 in Great Britain by
Society for Promoting Christian Knowledge
Holy Trinity Church
Marylebone Road
London NW1 4DU

This edition published 2002 in the United States of America by
Wm. B. Eerdmans Publishing Company
255 Jefferson Ave. S.E., Grand Rapids, Michigan 49503 /
P.O. Box 163 Cambridge CB3 9PU U.K.
www.eerdmans.com

Manufactured in Great Britain

06 05 04 03 02   5 4 3 2 1

ISBN 0–8028–3983–5

Contents

Contents

Preface

This book represents a return on my part to a subject that has absorbed much of my interest for the past twenty years, but its chronological approach makes it different from my earlier publications, and I hope that it offers fresh insights. It is written at a relatively popular level, and I have deliberately kept footnotes and bibliography to a bare minimum. I have, however, drawn extensively and gratefully on the ideas and insights of other scholars, and readers are referred to my earlier publications for full supporting bibliography.

I would like to thank all of those who have helped with the production of this book, particularly the staff and students of Wycliffe Hall, the former for allowing me sabbatical leave to write it and for their encouragement, the latter for sitting through lectures and tutorials in which various of the ideas have taken shape and been tried out. Various students read the manuscript: Mark Michael's comments were especially useful. I am grateful to the publishers SPCK and Eerdmans for taking the book on. And as always, I am particularly indebted to my wife Clare for her love and support and to my wider family, including Alan and Simon and my mother-in-law Joan Wilson.

I have enjoyed being part of the ministry team in a group of rural parishes near Oxford over the past seven years. I have among other things tried to make Jesus and Paul come alive through my teaching and preaching, and I hope this book, though addressing academic questions, will also help serve that purpose.

Introduction

'I would like to introduce you to Paul from Tarsus. You may have heard negative things about him, but I want to assure you that he is a fine man and a committed follower of Jesus Christ.' Such might well have been the gist of what Barnabas said to the apostles, when introducing Paul to them after Paul's conversion (Acts 9.27). The apostles and other Christians in Jerusalem were very nervous about the man who had been the arch-persecutor of the Church, but Barnabas believed in Paul and made the important introduction.

This book might be thought of as a twenty-first century attempt to do what Barnabas did. Many people today have a negative view of Paul: he is often accused of not being a faithful follower of Jesus, but a freelancer who did his own thing with the Christian religion. He is accused of changing Jesus' good ideas, and of introducing all sorts of bad ideas (for example, about women and sex); and he is often seen as an arrogant, self-opinionated man, with a rather tortuous theological mind. His failure to refer much to Jesus' earthly life and teaching in his letters has been thought to confirm that he was not really interested in the real Jesus, only in the quite different Jesus of his own theological imagination. I am convinced that this is a mistaken view of Paul, and in this book I hope to introduce him, and to tell something of 'the true story' of Paul and Jesus.

Our main sources of information about Paul are his own letters, which are found in the New Testament, and also the book of Acts, which is traditionally thought to have been written by Luke, one of Paul's companions. Modern scholars have had doubts about the New Testament documents and their reliability: some of the letters that are supposed to have been written by Paul are thought by some scholars to have been written by followers of Paul, not by Paul himself. As for Acts, some scholars see it as a romantic portrayal of the early Church rather than a reliable historical account. This book is not going to discuss these scholarly questions in technical detail; but we will need to bear them in mind when thinking about Paul's life. And indeed, if one main question being addressed in this book concerns the relationship of Paul and Jesus, another is the question of Acts and its portrait of Paul. We will be looking at Acts and Paul's letters side by side, and seeing what that comparison tells us.

In this book we will attempt to follow the story of Paul chronologically. In Part A we will try to piece together what we know of his origins and conversion. Then the bulk of the book, Part B, will focus attention on Paul's so-called missionary journeys and on four of his letters (Galatians, 1 and 2 Thessalonians and 1 Corinthians). In this part we will consider each of these letters in turn, looking first at its context, then at its contents, and finally at the light it sheds on the question of Paul and Jesus. In the final part we will look very briefly at other evidence, and draw some conclusions about Paul, about Paul and Jesus, and about Jesus.

The book is designed primarily for the ordinary reader and student, rather than for scholars, and I hope that it may be a helpful way into Paul for those who know little about him but who want to understand this most important and controversial of Christian saints and his early letters. It is not, on the other hand, a general introduction to Paul, but focuses on particular historical questions to do with the apostle. I hope that it makes a distinctive contribution to our understanding of Paul's early life and ministry and of his relationship to Jesus of Nazareth. Inevitably every chapter (notably those that attempt to summarize letters like Galatians and 1 Corinthians in a few pages!) leaves all sorts of questions unanswered. But I hope that, despite its deficiencies, the book's chronological approach and its attempt to view Paul's life, his letters and the Paul and Jesus question together will not only be novel, but also illuminating.

NOTE ON OTHER BOOKS

This book covers some similar ground to my earlier *Paul, Follower of Jesus or Founder of Christianity?* (Grand Rapids, Mich./Cambridge: Eerdmans, 1994). But its chronological approach and its attempt to correlate Acts and Paul's letters mean that it offers fresh perspectives. The earlier book gives much more detail and bibliographical information on the Paul and Jesus question than I can here. It compares the theological teaching and ideas of Jesus and Paul, investigates what Paul knew of Jesus, and considers different scholarly approaches to the issues. I looked at the question of Acts and Paul's letters in my article 'Acts and the Pauline Corpus II. The

Evidence of Parallels', in *The Book of Acts in its First Century Setting*, vol. 1, ed. B. W. Winter and A. D. Clarke (Carlisle: Paternoster, Grand Rapids: Eerdmans, 1993), 215–58.

There is a very large number of other works that could be mentioned. Professor F. F. Bruce was director of my doctoral studies at Manchester University, and his *Paul: Apostle of the Free Spirit* (Exeter: Paternoster, Grand Rapids: Eerdmans, 1977) is still a masterly account of Paul and his letters. A fellow student at Manchester was Colin Hemer, and his thesis, *The Book of Acts in the Setting of Hellenistic History* (Tübingen: Mohr, 1989), is a very valuable discussion of Acts. More recently, the series of volumes on *The Book of Acts in its First Century Setting* (Carlisle: Paternoster, Grand Rapids: Eerdmans, 1993 –) is a mine of information. R. Riesner's *Paul's Early Period* (Grand Rapids: Eerdmans, 1994) is a most impressive and detailed study of the chronological and other questions surrounding Paul's early life. Among the many fine commentaries on Acts that are available, B. Witherington's *The Acts of the Apostles: A Socio-Rhetorical Commentary* (Grand Rapids: Eerdmans, Carlisle: Paternoster, 1998) is full of useful up-to-date information. On the Pauline letters which we will be discussing, useful guides to further study include the following. On Galatians, see James D. G. Dunn, *The Theology of Paul's Letter to the Galatians* (Cambridge: Cambridge University Press, 1993); also John Barclay's *Obeying the Truth* (Edinburgh: T. & T. Clark, 1988). B. N. Longenecker's *Galatians* (Dallas: Word, 1990) is one of the various valuable commentaries available. On 1 and 2 Thessalonians, E. Best's *A Commentary on the First and Second Epistles to the Thessalonians* (London: Black, New York: Harper and Row, 1972) remains worthwhile, as does I. H. Marshall's *1 and 2 Thessalonians* (Grand Rapids: Eerdmans, 1983). On 1 Corinthians, James Dunn's *1 Corinthians* (Sheffield: Sheffield Academic Press, 1995) is a useful summary of the issues, and Bruce Winter's *Paul after Corinth* (Grand Rapids and Cambridge: Eerdmans, 2001) is a fresh and interesting book. The massive commentary by A. C. Thiselton, *The First Epistle to the Corinthians* (Carlisle: Paternoster, Grand Rapids: Eerdmans, 2000), will be too technical for some, but is thorough and important. Last but not least, Seyoon Kim's new book, *Paul and the New Perspective* (Grand Rapids: Eerdmans, 2001), is a significant scholarly discussion bearing directly on the Paul and Jesus question.

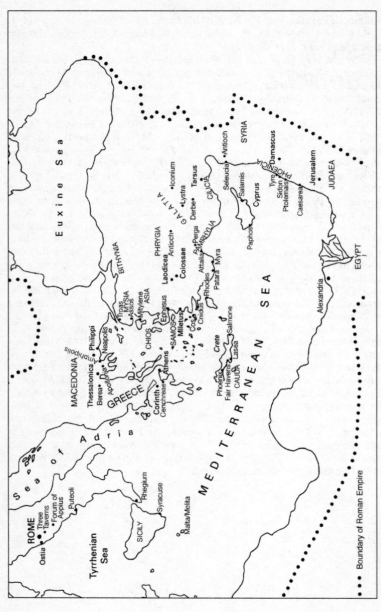

Paul's World

Boundary of Roman Empire

PART 1
BEGINNINGS

1 Before Paul met Jesus

What's your name and where do you come from?

Paul does not tell us much about his background in his letters; why
should he? But we do know

- his name – Paulos. It was a common Graeco-Roman name.
- that he came from a practising Jewish family: 'circumcised on the
  eighth day, of the people of Israel, of the tribe of Benjamin, a
  Hebrew born of Hebrews, as to the law a Pharisee' (Philippians
  3.5).
- that as an adult, he had a trade 'working with his hands'
  (1 Corinthians 4.12; 1 Thessalonians 2.9).

All of this fits in with what the book of Acts tells us, though Acts
fills out the picture much more. It confirms that his name was Paul,
though at first it calls him 'Saul', a Hebrew name. The probability is
that like many other Jewish children he had a Hebrew name and a
Roman name; it makes sense that a Jewish child from the tribe of
Benjamin might have been called Saul after Israel's first king, who
came from the tribe of Benjamin (1 Samuel 9). Perhaps the family
chose the Roman name Paul partly because it sounded like his
Hebrew name!

Acts tells us that Saul/Paul was born in Tarsus, 'no mean city', as
Paul is said to have commented (Acts 21.39). It was a large,
prosperous city – someone has estimated its population as half a
million people, which was very big for those days. It was known for
its educational and philosophical schools. It had a well-established
Jewish quarter. It was ten miles from the sea up the river Cnydus, in
what is now south Turkey.

Paul's letters do not directly confirm his origins in Tarsus, but
they do speak of him spending a lot of time in that general area after
his conversion (Galatians 1.21 and the rest of Galatians). His
fluency in Greek and familiarity with Greek rhetoric fit with his
being a Jew, whose first language was probably Aramaic ('a Hebrew

3

of the Hebrews'), but who was very much at home in a Greek-speaking environment.

Acts agrees that Paul was a Pharisee, and speaks of him being brought up in Jerusalem 'at the feet of Gamaliel' (22.3). Gamaliel was probably the most notable Jewish rabbi in Jerusalem in the New Testament period, and seems to have been relatively liberal in his views. Some people have doubted whether the extremist-firebrand Saul, as he turned out to be, could have come from Gamaliel's moderate school, but anyone teaching in a college today knows that the students are often far more militant than their teachers!

Acts tells us that Paul's profession was tent-making (or leather-working, more generally), and also that he was born a Roman citizen. Roman citizenship was a privileged status only granted to some people in the empire, and we don't know how or why Paul's family acquired citizenship. A number of the famous Roman generals, including Julius Caesar and Mark Antony, visited Tarsus, and it is quite likely that one of Paul's family earned their favour, or the favour of the great emperor Augustus. The suggestion that his father earned citizenship by making tents for the Roman army is speculation, and it is possible that Paul actually took up tent-making after his conversion, when he was presumably cut off from his family and his previous support-base. Various factors, including his Roman citizenship, his studies under Gamaliel, and then his appointment as leader of the anti-Christian campaign of the Jerusalem religious authorities, all suggest that he came from a rather influential Jewish family, with friends in high places. So becoming a Christian and turning his back on all of that represented a big 'loss' for him (Philippians 3.8, 9).

His letters do not confirm all the details from Acts. He speaks not of his Roman citizenship, but of the Christian's heavenly citizenship (Philippians 3.20). However, the impression we get from his letters is of a competent, confident leader, who was able to relate to all sorts of people, and this fits well with what Acts tells us about his background.

We know very little indeed of his family: he speaks at one point of some relatives who were Christians before him and who are in prison in Rome (Romans 16.7, an intriguing reference); Acts refers to a sister of Paul in Jerusalem, and to her son, who seems to have had contacts in high places; interestingly he helps Paul (Acts 23.16). Some people have wondered if Paul was married and then widowed or divorced, perhaps when he was converted; but, although some Christians in the second or third centuries believed him to have been married (probably misunderstanding 'true yokefellow' in Philippians 4.3: cf. Clement of Alexandria, *Stromateis* III.vi.53; Ignatius, *Philadelphiaus* 4.4 or 44), there is no hard evidence for this. It is true that Jewish men would normally have married, but Paul was a 'young man' at the time of the stoning of Stephen, according to Acts (7.58), quite likely still a student. (Some have argued that he was a member of the Sanhedrin, the supreme Jewish Council, since Acts 26.10 refers to him 'casting his vote' against the Christians; but it is most unlikely that he was one of the elders on the Council. More likely he was one of the students who attended the sessions of the Council.) It would not be a great surprise if this angry young man was not yet married when he got very actively involved in opposing the Christian movement.

If Paul was between 15 and 20 in the early 30s AD when Stephen was martyred, then he would have been born in Tarsus between AD 15 and 20 (and, looking ahead, this would mean that he was in his forties when writing a letter like 1 Corinthians). How long he stayed in Tarsus before coming to Jerusalem for his Pharisaic education is impossible to say. But it is at least possible that he was in Jerusalem before the death of Jesus, and indeed at the same time as Jesus.

Paul's first contacts with Jesus and his followers

Although Paul may well have been in Jerusalem at the same time as Jesus, there is no evidence that he met or heard Jesus. When he refers to 'seeing the Lord' in 1 Corinthians 9.1 he almost certainly is referring to meeting the risen Jesus at the time of his conversion (cf. 1 Corinthians 15.7). It might seem a little surprising that he did not see Jesus before then; but the gospels suggest that Jesus came to Jerusalem just for festivals, and it has been estimated that at festival times there could have been one hundred thousand pilgrims in the city (on top of the usual population, which one scholar has calculated at about 30,000). There is no reason why the young Pharisee student Saul, even if he was in Jerusalem at the same time as Jesus, should have had any contact with him. I am reminded of how often royalty and religious leaders visit Oxford, where I live (with its population of about 120,000), and I hardly ever get to see them, even if I know they are around! Even if Saul knew that Jesus was in town, he might have deliberately chosen to keep away from this young teacher of whom the Pharisees so strongly disapproved!

The first recorded contact between Saul and the Christian movement was when Stephen was stoned. Acts says that those stoning Stephen 'laid their clothes at the feet of a young man named Saul'; then, after describing the stoning, it says, 'And Saul was there, giving approval to his death' (7.58; 8.1). It goes on immediately to describe a massive persecution of the Jerusalem church, and comments: 'Saul began to destroy the church. Going from house to house, he dragged off men and women and put them in prison' (8.3).

This account dovetails very well with Paul's own account of his early and hostile relations with Christians. Thus in Galatians 1.13 he comments, 'you have heard of my previous way of life in Judaism, how intensely I persecuted the church of God and tried to destroy it. I was advancing in Judaism beyond many Jews of my own age and was extremely zealous for the traditions of my fathers.' He refers also to his persecution of the Church in 1 Corinthians 15.9, and in Philippians 3.5–6, saying that he was 'in regard to the law, a Pharisee; as for zeal, persecuting the church' (cf. 1 Timothy 1.13).

Acts and Paul's letters agree that he was a zealous young Pharisee, who saw it as his religious duty to stamp out the fast-growing Christian movement and who was ruthless in trying to do so.

Paul does not refer to Stephen. But Acts' account of Paul and Stephen is entirely plausible. Stephen was one of the seven men who were appointed to help with the early Church's feeding programme. According to Acts the earliest Christian church had a strong community life, the rich sharing their wealth with the poor and food being given to the very poor, especially to widows (one of the most vulnerable groups in ancient society) (5.32–37). However, in the rapidly expanding early church the administration of this practical help programme was going awry, and in particular complaints came from the Greek-speaking widows that they were being neglected (6.1–3). So the seven were appointed to oversee the efficient and fair distribution of food. They have often been seen as the first 'deacons' of the Christian church; the word 'deacon' means literally 'servant', and the seven were chosen to take responsibility for 'serving' at tables (6.2).

Interestingly the seven all have Greek names, and it looks as though they were appointed not just to do a practical job, but also in recognition of the importance of the Greek-speaking minority in the growing Church. It is likely that Jesus and the twelve apostles mainly spoke Aramaic (though they probably also spoke Greek, and perhaps Hebrew and Latin as well), and that the church in Jerusalem was Aramaic-speaking to start with. But there were large numbers of Jews in different parts of the Roman Empire, for whom Greek was their mother tongue. Some of these had settled in Jerusalem, and some of these became Christians. The seven appear to have come from these Greek-speakers, and they seem to have been not just backroom administrators, but people who took a lead in the development of the church's work among Greek-speakers. So Stephen is described as having dealings with 'the synagogue of the freedmen (as it was called)', and with Jews who came from Cyrene and Alexandria (in North Africa) and from Cilicia and Asia (in Turkey, as we know it today) (6.9). Philip, another of the seven, is said to have taken the good news to Samaria, and also to an Ethiopian (Acts 8).

Although Paul does not refer to Stephen, it is plausible that there was some link between the two men: Paul came from Tarsus in Cilicia, and, although he was himself a 'Hebrew of the Hebrews' speaking Aramaic, he was also entirely at home in Greek, and might very well have been in touch with a synagogue which included people from his home area. The book of Acts also suggests that Stephen was seen, at least by his enemies, to have been critical of the temple and the law of Moses (6.13, 14). We may guess that, like Jesus, he was critical of the Pharisaic emphasis on details of the Jewish law and of the mystique often associated with the temple, both tending to blind people to the priorities and purposes of God. (Stephen's speech in Acts 7 points in that direction.) But, whatever his exact position, it makes excellent sense that the young Pharisee student Saul would have seen the up-and-coming Christian leader Stephen and what he stood for as highly offensive and dangerous, and that Stephen may have been a significant catalyst leading Saul to take an active and eventually a leading role in the campaign against the Christian movement. One small point of interest is that the book of Acts says slightly mysteriously that the persecution of the Christians following the death of Stephen led to the scattering of the Jerusalem Christians throughout Judaea and Samaria, 'except for the apostles' (8.1). It seems odd that the apostles were exempted, unless the persecution was precisely aimed at the Greek-speaking Christians such as Stephen and Philip (whose story follows immediately in Acts).

It is an attractive thought that Stephen was not only influential in making Paul a persecutor of the Church, but also an inspiration to Paul after his conversion. Did Paul take up Stephen's mantle as a leader in the Greek-speaking church and also take forward Stephen's critique of Pharisaic and other Jewish attitudes to the law and the temple? I had thought of entitling this book *Paul Follows Jesus*, but it might be true also to say that 'Paul follows Stephen'. But first Paul had to get converted.

2 The big bang!

The story of Paul's meeting with the risen Jesus on the Damascus Road must be the most famous conversion story of all time. However we understand the event, it changed the world – and not just for Paul himself. It did, of course, change Paul's world. Some people have questioned whether it should be called a 'conversion', since in Paul's view it was not a case of changing his religion, but of finding the Messiah for whom he and other Jews had been waiting. However, if the word 'conversion' means turning from one way to another, that certainly happened to Paul. It was a dramatic change. In 2 Corinthians 5.17 Paul can use the phrase 'new creation' of the person who becomes a Christian. It was like that for him: the light that shone at creation shone into his heart, and brought new life (2 Corinthians 4.3). It also brought a whole new understanding of God and his purposes: when Paul says in Galatians 1.12 that he received his gospel 'by revelation from Jesus Christ', he is clearly referring to his conversion as the momentous occasion when he came to understand the good news.

It all happened when he was leading an anti-Christian campaign. There had been a campaign going on against the Christian movement for some time: the arrest and execution of Jesus in around AD 30 was the first main attempt to eliminate the troublesome movement, as the authorities saw it. But unfortunately for them this did not stop the Christian momentum for any length of time; indeed rather the opposite happened. The Christians claimed that Jesus had come to life again, and the authorities found themselves faced with a rapidly growing movement of people, who were not only propagating the ideas that had made Jesus so offensive but were also claiming that the authorities had disgracefully executed someone who had now been brought to life again by God and who was the Jewish Messiah.

There seem to have been sporadic attempts to stop the progress of the emerging Church, but things seem to have taken a more violent turn with Stephen, as we have seen. Whether this was because he was more vocal in his criticism of Jewish religion than the twelve apostles had been, or whether it was that the Jewish leaders were getting more desperate as they saw the 'heresy' spreading from the original Galilean-led group to other Jewish groups, or whether it was particular individuals who became involved in the anti-Christian campaign, we don't know. But certainly one very forceful individual got involved, namely the young Pharisaic student Saul.

The impact on the Christian movement of the persecution that followed Stephen's martyrdom was dramatic. But once again the effect was more positive than negative, from a Christian point of view, as the Christians who were forced to leave Jerusalem spread the message to all sorts of places (Acts 8.1, 4). Damascus in Syria was one of the places which soon had a group of Christians associated with the Jewish synagogues there. From the point of view of the Jerusalem authorities, the situation was alarming; the cancer was spreading across the Jewish world, corrupting Jews and also, no doubt, Gentile 'God-fearing' supporters of the synagogue. In this context Saul was authorized to pursue the Christians in Damascus; we may guess that this was his initiative, which was then approved by the authorities.

All of this is spelled out by the book of Acts, but Paul's letter to the Galatians confirms that he was a zealous persecutor of the Christians, and that his conversion took place in or near Damascus (1.13–15). As for a date: these developments may well have taken place within a year or two of the death of Jesus, and so Saul was on the Damascus Road in AD 31 or 32. (For a scholarly discussion of all dating issues see R. Riesner, *Paul's Early Period*.)

What was Paul thinking as he went to Damascus?

Who knows exactly what Paul was thinking as he went on that fateful journey? It would be unwise to speculate too much. On the other hand, we can be reasonably confident about various things. He must have thought that the Christian movement was pernicious and needed stamping out, and he must have thought that it was God's will that this should happen. More precisely, we can consider this question under the following four sub-headings.

What will Paul have thought about Jesus?

He must have known something, probably quite a lot, about Jesus, especially if he had been engaged in furious debate with people like Stephen. He will have known that Jesus was a popular religious leader, with a following in Galilee, who claimed that God's deliverance of his people, promised in the Old Testament, was coming in and through his ministry. He will have known of Jesus' supposed miracles of healing and exorcism: they were acclaimed by his followers as divinely inspired signs, but rejected by Paul and other Pharisees as bogus or as demon-inspired.

He will have known of the Christians' claim that Jesus was the Messiah, God's chosen leader; but presumably he saw Jesus as a false prophet, guilty of misleading the people. In particular he will have objected to Jesus' apparent laxity towards the Old Testament law, and his carelessness about purity. The Pharisees were famous for detailed observance of the law, and for their attempts to separate themselves from anything unclean or impure – the name 'Pharisee' may well have meant 'separatist' originally. They wanted to keep the Jewish nation holy and distinctive at a time when foreign influences were very strong. Jesus in some ways seemed to be pulling in the opposite direction, claiming to be from God, but taking a relaxed view of the sabbath and mixing freely with people who were known sinners. Paul will have objected to Jesus on these grounds. He will also very likely have objected to Jesus' provocative words and actions in relation to the temple; Jesus' driving out of the traders and his predictions of the temple's destruction were seen as an arrogant insult to the most sacred institution of Judaism.

Paul will have known the Christian tales about Jesus' having risen from the dead, but have emphatically rejected them; he was clear that Jesus was dead, duly executed for his sins. The Old Testament book of Deuteronomy spoke of prophets who do miraculous signs but lead people away from the true worship of God, and commanded that they be put to death (13.1–5). The same book of Deuteronomy also describes what to do with the bodies of those who have been executed by hanging, and says that they must not be left hanging overnight, 'because anyone who is hung on a tree is under God's curse' (21.22–3). We may guess that Paul the Pharisee

11

will have taken these laws very seriously, and have seen Jesus as deserving death for misleading the people.

What was Paul's view of the law and of how to be right with God?

As we have implied, Paul was motivated by 'zeal for the law' (Galatians 3.14, Philippians 3.5,6). Like the writer of Psalm 119 (e.g. vv. 9–11), Paul will have regarded the law of God not as a burden, but as God's gift to his people and as the way to live a righteous life pleasing to God. He, like other Pharisees, saw it as his vocation to help people keep the law. Of course, he also believed in the grace and love of God towards Israel; but keeping the law was the way to remain in that love, and not to fall under the judgement of God.

What will Paul have thought about himself and his standing before God?

It seems clear that he was a very scrupulous, law-keeping Pharisaic Jew, and in Philippians 3.6 he can even refer to himself as 'blameless under the law' – before his conversion. In attacking the Christians he will have seen himself as upholding God's law and religious purity, in the face of Christian laxity. And presumably he thought of himself, with some justification, as righteous before God. Not that he will have thought of himself as perfect in every respect, but he will have seen himself, understandably, as a member of God's chosen people and as a particularly righteous one; he was a high scorer religiously, setting a good example to others. Jesus' parable of the Pharisee and the tax collector in Luke 18.9–14 may be deliberately caricaturing Pharisaic attitudes, with the Pharisee thanking God 'that I am not like all other men – robbers, evildoers, adulterers – or even like this tax collector. I fast twice a week and give a tenth of all I get'. And yet it is not unlikely that Paul might have been similarly thankful for his religious achievements. Not that he was complacent; he was pursuing what he saw as the way of righteousness, fiercely.

What was Paul's attitude to Christians and to Gentiles?

He will have seen the Gentiles as outside the people of God and as unclean sinners, from whom faithful Jews should keep separate. As for the Christians, they had been misled by Jesus, and were misleading others. Paul will have objected to their proclamation of Jesus as Messiah, to the liberalism of some of them towards the Jewish law, and to their increasing association with non-Jews, such as Samaritans. One especially worrying development was the way the Christian heresy was spreading internationally. The Christians needed urgently to be brought to heel, before the contagion got out of control.

Whether Paul would have expressed his views in exactly these terms cannot be proved. But it is not fanciful to suggest that that is roughly how he is likely to have seen things as he travelled up the Damascus Road.

But then came the conversion.

Paul's dramatic conversion

We have three different accounts of Paul's conversion in the book of Acts (chs. 9, 22 and 26), and Paul refers to it himself in Galatians 1. The accounts in Acts vary slightly (which doesn't seem to worry the author of Acts, and need not worry us!), but the general picture is the same. This is how Acts 9 describes it:

> As he neared Damascus on his journey, suddenly a light from heaven flashed around him. He fell to the ground and heard a voice say to him, 'Saul, Saul, why do you persecute me?' 'Who are you, Lord?' Saul asked. 'I am Jesus, whom you are persecuting,' he replied. 'Now get up and go into the city, and you will be told what you must do.' The men travelling with Saul stood there speechless; they heard the sound but did not see anyone. Saul got up from the ground, but when he opened his eyes he could see nothing. So they led him by the hand into Damascus. For three days he was blind, and did not eat or drink anything. (vv. 3–9)

Paul in his letters does not describe his conversion in this sort of detail; but he does mention it. In Galatians 1.15–17 he speaks of being a persecutor of the Church, to whom God 'revealed his Son', and there is a clear hint that this happened in the Damascus area. He speaks elsewhere of having 'seen the Lord' after his resurrection and of having seen 'the glory of God in the face of Christ'

(1 Corinthians 9.1; 15.8–10; 2 Corinthians 4.6). Acts does not tell us specifically that Paul saw Jesus, but he saw an amazing, indeed blinding, light which clearly emanated from Jesus, who then spoke to him. Paul does not tell us of his conversation with the risen Christ, but he does tell us that his revelatory experience was to lead to his commissioning as a preacher to the Gentiles (Galatians 1.15; Acts 26.17).

Paul's evidence and the Acts stories are entirely compatible with each other, and they agree on the main lines of what Paul experienced. There are, however, all sorts of questions that intrigue modern readers. For example, how exactly should we understand Paul's experience? Was it a subjective experience within Paul's mind? Acts suggests not, observing that Paul's companions saw the light and/or heard a sound, though they did not know what was going on. Was it a totally unexpected experience? Or had Paul been moved and even persuaded by Stephen and others before this event, but without admitting it? Such speculations about Paul's subconscious are, of course, totally unprovable one way or the other. What is not speculation is that Paul had this experience of the risen Jesus, as he saw it, and that it turned much of his thinking upside down.

What happened to Paul's ideas as a result of his conversion?

What happened to his view of Jesus?

Far from being a dead false prophet, Jesus turns out to be magnificently alive. The Christians had been right in seeing him as the Messiah; Paul has now experienced him in blinding, divine glory. Paul's letters speak of Jesus as Lord, as Son of God, as the image of God (1 Corinthians 11.7); how much of this Paul grasped at the time of his conversion or immediately after it we have no way of knowing. But it is not unlikely that he will have grasped much immediately.

As for the death of Jesus, no longer could Paul think that Jesus deserved death for misleading the people. The glorious Lord, whom he had now met, could not possibly have been crucified either for his own sins, or just by unfortunate accident. There must have been some deep divine purpose in his death. The conclusion Paul came to was that Jesus' death was not for his own sins, but for the sins of others.

As a well-taught Jew Paul was familiar with the idea of death bringing salvation. Thus:

- the greatest Jewish festival, Passover, celebrated the liberating (or 'redemption') of God's people from slavery through the killing of a lamb (Exodus 12);
- the Old Testament sacrificial system had at its heart – the idea of forgiveness of sin through the death of an animal. One of the most important days in the Jewish calendar was the Day of Atonement, when the high priest took the blood of a sacrificial animal into the holiest place in the temple to make atonement for the sins of the people (eg Leviticus 4—5, 16);
- the book of Isaiah spoke of the people in Israel being in exile for their sins, but then of the Lord's servant taking the people's punishment on himself – so that they might be put right with God and go free (Isaiah 52—53);
- more recently in Jewish history, the Jews saw some of the Maccabee heroes who gave their lives in the third and second centuries BC as martyrs whose deaths had atoning power (e.g. 4 Maccabees 17.21–23).

Given these ideas, it is not difficult to see how Paul came sooner or later to the conclusion that Jesus 'died for our sins' and to bring liberation, atonement and justification (1 Corinthians 15.3, compare 5.7–8, 1.30, Romans 3.24–26). Paul came to see the cross as the supreme evidence of God's love and as God's way of reconciling the world to himself (2 Corinthians 5.14–21, Romans 5.6–8, 8.32).

What happened to his view of the law and of how to be right with God?

In a real sense we could say that the law took a knock through Paul's conversion experience. He had seen it as the flawless guide to living according to the will of God, and believed himself to have been doing God's will by his zeal for the law. But in fact his zeal for the law had led him up the Damascus Road. The law had not proved to be the route to salvation or to pleasing God, but had instead been hijacked by sin and had led him in totally the wrong direction. Paul does not conclude that the law is evil; far from it – it represents the holy and good way of God (Romans 7.12). But the law is very much demoted in his thinking, and before long he will be opposing those who are zealous for the law in the way that he was before his conversion.

What happened to his view of himself and of the way to salvation?

Paul had believed that he was a righteous person doing God's will, but now he found out that by his campaigning against the Christians he was actually persecuting God's Messiah – the one sent by God to save his people – and opposing the messianic mission. It must have been a devastating discovery, as if an advanced driver, who prides himself on his road sense and driving skills, suddenly finds himself driving the wrong way down a dual carriageway. Far from being righteous Paul now discovered himself to be guilty of the most heinous of sins.

It was a devastating but illuminating discovery. It was illuminating negatively. First, because he discovered that someone can be fervently religious, but sincerely and seriously wrong (Romans 10.2: 'they are zealous for God, but their zeal is not based on knowledge'). And second because he discovered the subtlety of sin. Paul speaks in his letter to the Romans about sin's sinfulness being revealed in the way 'it produced death in me through what was good' (7.13). That is generally true: sin takes good things like science or sex, and uses them for evil destructive purposes (e.g. nuclear weapons and child abuse). But Paul's point is to do with the law of God – something very good, given to Israel by God; and yet sin got in, and Paul's zeal for the law actually led Paul to persecute the Messiah. Paul was not neurotic about sin, but realistic, because his own painful experience had taught him how subtle and sinister its destructive work can be.

But, if Paul learned negative things about sin, he also learned positive things about the grace of God. It was now blindingly clear that the way to be right with God was not via extreme enthusiasm for the law. Salvation was in fact a totally undeserved gift of God. That is what he experienced on the Damascus Road: he was a fanatical enemy of Christ and the Christians, but Christ met him and called him, astonishingly and quite undeservedly. Paul thus discovered grace in a way that he had never discovered it before. Of course, as a Jew he had the concept of God's grace choosing Israel, and of himself as one of that chosen people. He did not, however, see himself as a great sinner, but as one who was pleasing to God because of his law-keeping. Now that was changed: he was the greatest of sinners (a phrase actually found in 1 Timothy 2.14–16), saved not by his law-keeping but by the mercy of God. He experienced the astonishing fact that the Son of God 'loved me and gave himself for me' (Galatians 2.20).

Paul's zeal for God was not diminished through his conversion; rather the opposite. But his arrogance was eliminated by his discovery of himself as a sinner, and was replaced by gratitude; and his zeal was redirected and its focus was not now on the law, but on the grace of God shown in the death of Jesus.

What happened to his view of Christians and Gentiles?

What happened on the Damascus Road was a dramatic intervention by the risen Jesus on the side of the Christians. (According to Acts, Jesus very explicitly identified himself with his followers, saying to Paul, 'Saul, Saul, why do you persecute me?': 9.4; 22.7; 26.14.) Astonishingly, from Paul's point of view, the Christians were after all God's faithful people: they had rightly recognized Jesus as God's Messiah, and Jesus by his intervention had unmistakably identified the Church as his people. As for the Gentiles, whom he had regarded as unclean sinners and beyond the pale, Paul's discovery of his own sin and of divine grace meant that no longer could he think of Jews as righteous and of Gentiles as sinners outside the reach of God's love. If God's love could reach him, a Pharisee persecutor of the Church, that love could surely reach other 'sinners', including the Gentiles.

Paul sensed that he was being called by the risen Jesus to go to the Gentiles (cf. Galatians 1.15; Acts 9.15). If you are on your way from Jerusalem to Damascus, and God intervenes in your life so dramatically, you might well conclude that God has some special purpose for your life. Paul concluded that his calling was not to persecute Christians, but to take the good news of Christ from Jerusalem into the Gentile world. He knew that the Old Testament promised salvation to Israel, but it also contained hints and promises that the Gentiles would be brought in (e.g. Isaiah 42.6,

49.6). Paul believed that he was called to gather in the Gentile 'outsiders' (Romans 15.8–20).

It is important to say that Paul may not have instantaneously worked out all the points that we have made at the time when he was converted. However, we should not underestimate how creative an experience his conversion must have been, given his background. Not that he was the first to come to all these conclusions: even before he became a Christian, he will have known the Christians' ideas about Jesus dying 'for our sins' (1 Corinthians 15.3), and the Christian traditions about Jesus mixing with sinners and offering them God's salvation (e.g. Luke 15.1,2). But it was his own conversion experience that brought these things home to him, in such a way that he can insist that the gospel which he preached was not man's gospel, nor taught by man, but came by revelation from God (Galatians 1.11, 12). Key ingredients in his theology – his view of Jesus, of the law, of sin, of grace, of the Church, of the Gentiles – were all given him on that fateful day. The importance of the experience for Paul may be confirmed by the book of Acts, since Paul tells the story both to the Jews and to the Romans, in order to explain himself and to defend his later actions (Acts 22, 24).

It was a 'big bang' for Paul – shaking up all his previous ideas, but hugely creative for his theology and ministry in the years that followed.

3 New directions

It is hard to imagine how deep the shock of what had happened to him must have been for Paul and how humiliating it must have been for the once-proud Pharisee to come into Damascus, helpless and blind. Things had not turned out as planned, to say the least!

Ananias

But Acts describes a Christian 'disciple', Ananias, being sent by God to Paul (9.10–19). Acts suggests that Ananias was scared, because Paul's reputation as a brutal persecutor of the Church had preceded him. It is not unlikely that some of those whom he had persecuted in Jerusalem had fled to Damascus, and it must have been terrifying to hear that their arch-enemy had come with a body of men to pursue them. The Christians might understandably have been slow to believe that Paul's professed conversion was genuine; could it all be a clever trap that he was setting? Despite his fears, Ananias went to Paul, placed his hands on him, and addressed him (strikingly) as 'Brother Saul'. Through his ministry Paul's eyesight was restored, and he was baptized. We are not told any details of his baptism, but it must have been extraordinary for the man who had so opposed Christians and Christian baptism to go down into the water, confessing Jesus as Lord, and now to be part of the Christian community.

Paul does not tell us anything about Ananias in his letters, which is hardly surprising since in the letters we have he only alludes to his conversion. Some people have thought that his insistence in Galatians that he did not receive his gospel from any man (1.12) tells against the Acts story. But that statement cannot be taken to mean that Paul learned nothing of Jesus from any human being at all: Paul must have learned things from the Christians he persecuted (even if he did not agree with them then), and he tells us in other parts of his writings that he 'received' Christian traditions (1 Corinthians 11.23; 15.3); this is something we shall look at in more

19

detail later. No, when he says that he received his gospel or good news direct from God, he is referring to the way that his conversion was decisive in convincing him of key things such as the Lordship of Jesus and salvation by grace not the law. He is not denying that people like Ananias had an important part to play.

What happened next?

In Acts

Acts suggests the sequence of events listed below.

1. Paul stayed some time in Damascus, and instead of persecuting Christians he started preaching and teaching about Jesus in the Jewish synagogues – to the astonishment of people who knew his previous reputation.

2. His powerful advocacy of the Christian cause infuriated the Jews, who plotted to kill him. Such an extreme reaction may seem strange to us, and yet we know that Paul himself had just been murderously hostile to the Christians. And we know how religious feelings can still run very high and lead to actual or threatened violence, for example against the novelist Salman Rushdie. The Jews had much more reason to hate Paul than modern Muslims to hate Rushdie: he was a traitor who did not keep his conversion secret, but went from being a leading defender of Judaism against the Christians to being a leading advocate of Christianity 'against' the Jews. He was inevitably disturbing the Jewish community, drawing people after him (Acts 9.25 speaks of Paul's followers); it quite probably looked to the Jews as though the one who was previously trying to destroy the Christian movement was now trying to destroy them. No wonder they plotted against him. Paul, Acts tells us, had to escape from Damascus, being lowered over the walls in a basket – an indignity of the first order for the one who had come with the sanction of the Jerusalem authorities.

3. From Damascus he went to Jerusalem, and tried to meet up with the Christians in Jerusalem. Acts tells us that they were very nervous of him, 'not believing that he really was a disciple' (9.26). Their fear was understandable, given that the

last time he was in Jerusalem he had been such a fierce attacker of the Church. They may have heard of his conversion, but could they be sure that that was genuine? In any case it will not have been easy to welcome someone who had been so cruel and fearsome.

At this point Barnabas enters Paul's story. Acts has already described 'Joseph, a Levite from Cyprus, whom the apostles called Barnabas (which means Son of Encouragement)' as a man of conspicuous generosity. He had donated a field to the Church earlier on, to help its programme of aid to the poor (4.36, 37). Now his generosity of spirit and his encouraging nature come to the fore again, as he evidently befriends Paul and reassures the Christians in Jerusalem of the sincerity of his conversion, bringing Paul to the apostles.

4. Paul then involved himself in Christian witness in Jerusalem, 'speaking boldly in the name of the Lord'. In particular he debated with the 'Greek-speakers'. It sounds as though he has taken on something of the role of Stephen. Once again his own position has been completely reversed: he had been the leading Jewish opponent of the Greek-speaking Christians; now he is their vigorous defender. It is not surprising that once again his life is under threat, and that there is a plot to kill the traitor. Once again Paul is rescued by his Christian brothers, and he is shipped right out of Palestine to Tarsus, his home city (9.26–30).

Such is the story in Acts.

In Galatians

Galatians gives a rather different picture (1.16–24). Here Paul says that after Jesus' appearance to him,

> I did not consult any man, nor did I go up to Jerusalem to see those who were apostles before I was, but I went immediately into Arabia, and later returned to Damascus. Then after three years, I went up to Jerusalem to get acquainted with Peter and stayed with him fifteen days. I saw none of the other apostles – only James, the Lord's brother. I assure you before God that what I am writing to you is no lie. Later I went to Syria and Cilicia. I was

21

personally unknown to the churches of Judea that are in Christ. They only heard the report: 'The man who formerly persecuted us is now preaching the faith he once tried to destroy.' And they praised God because of me.

In Acts and Galatians

At first sight the accounts in Acts and Galatians seem significantly different:

- Galatians talks about a period of years before Paul came up to Jerusalem, Acts of 'days';
- Galatians mentions Paul spending time in Arabia, Acts doesn't;
- Galatians suggests that Paul's visit to Jerusalem was rather private and only involved him meeting Peter and James, the brother of Jesus, but Acts suggests that he met the apostles as a group and that he had a public ministry in Jerusalem.

Some scholars see these discrepancies as evidence that Acts is historically inaccurate. However, the conclusion is unjustified; two points should be noted.

First, Acts and Galatians agree on the general order and pattern of events: Paul is converted in or near Damascus; he goes up to Jerusalem after quite some time ('many days' according to Acts 9.23, three years according to Galatians 1.18); he is not there very long, but goes on to Tarsus in Cilicia and then later to Antioch in Syria, according to Acts (9.38, 11.25), or to Syria and Cilicia according to Galatians (1.21).

Second, Paul in Galatians is giving a rather detailed chronological account of his movements after his conversion and of his contacts with Jerusalem, because of critics who argued that he was a second-hand apostle dependent on Jerusalem. (We will come back to this point in Chapter 6.) Acts 9 tells us of Paul's conversion in the context of describing the story of the Jerusalem church and its expansion; so its description of what happened immediately after Paul's conversion is understandably abbreviated, focusing on the impact of his conversion on the church in Jerusalem and the surrounding areas.

There is therefore no problem with Acts' failure to mention the visit to Arabia; it can perfectly well be fitted in between the 'several days' of Acts 9.19 and the 'many days' of 9.23. There is at best a minor discrepancy between Acts' general reference to Paul being introduced to 'the apostles' and Paul's more specific information that he met Peter and James. As for Acts saying that he had a public ministry, particularly with the Greek-speakers, and Galatians saying that he was not even known to the churches of Judaea, there is again no great problem: if Paul only stayed in Jerusalem for a short time, as he suggests in Galatians – fifteen days with Peter, according to Galatians 1.18 – we do not need much imagination to guess that this was because his life was very soon at risk in Jerusalem; otherwise he would surely have stayed much longer. It may surprise us that he came back at all, or that he risked any public ministry, since he must have known that he was one of the most hated people in Jerusalem. On the other hand, it is also hard to imagine the man who had had that extraordinary life-changing experience on the Damascus Road not wanting to witness in those circles where previously he had been so violent a persecutor; he was willing to risk all sorts of equally dangerous things later in his ministry (see 2 Corinthians 11.23–29). So it makes sense that he witnessed to them; it makes sense that he did not last long and had to be shipped out; it makes sense that he did not have time to get well known in the Christian churches of Judaea.

One small confirmation of the Acts story could be 1 Thessalonians 2.14, 15, where Paul speaks of the churches of Judaea and of the Jews who persecuted them. He comments that they 'killed the Lord Jesus and the prophets and also drove us out'; if 1 Thessalonians is correctly dated to AD 49, then Paul's remark about being 'driven out' by the Jews could be referring to Paul's first visit back to Jerusalem after his conversion, as described by Acts. On the other hand, it could be that Paul is referring here to his more recent experiences in Thessalonica itself.

The conclusion is that Acts and Galatians are quite different accounts of what happened after Paul's conversion, but almost entirely complementary to each other, each throwing light on the other.

In Arabia

One intriguing question remains: what did Paul do in Arabia? In Galatians he tells us that he went there straight after his conversion. It is tempting to think of this as something like Jesus' time of temptation in the desert, not least because Arabia suggests a place full of deserts to us! Did Paul go to Arabia to reflect on what had happened to him, and to start sorting out his life and his thinking? After all the traumas he had just been through, it would have made sense to get away for a while.

However, Arabia as referred to by Paul is not Arabia in our modern sense, but may well refer to the kingdom of Nabatea, just south-east of Palestine. The king of Nabatea at the time was Aretas IV, and in 2 Corinthians 11.32–3 Paul refers to how 'In Damascus the ethnarch [governor] under King Aretas had the city of the Damascenes guarded in order to arrest me. But I was lowered in a basket from a window in the wall and slipped through his hands.' This verse is very intriguing. On the one hand it seems to fit in both with Galatians, where Paul refers to his time in Arabia, and with Acts, which refers to his being let down over the walls of Damascus in a basket; it therefore confirms that detail in Acts. On the other hand, it raises questions:

- Acts suggests that the Jews, not Aretas, were after Paul and compelled his undignified escape from the city. Is Acts mistaken at this point?
- Why was the ethnarch of the king of Nabatea out to get Paul? Does this suggest that Paul did not just meditate in Nabatea, but was involved in effective ministry, thus stirring up some hostility in royal circles? Should we regard this as Paul's first 'missionary journey'?
- But in any case what was an ethnarch of King Aretas doing in Damascus?

It is difficult, and perhaps impossible, to answer these questions. It could possibly be that Damascus was under Nabatean rule at the time; Aretas IV was a successful king (under the Romans) who ruled from 9 or 8 BC to AD 40; the splendour of his rule is illustrated by the lion-griffin temple at Petra in present-day Jordan. But it may more simply be that there were Jewish and Nabatean quarters in the city of Damascus, and that the Jews and Nabateans collaborated in trying to get rid of Paul. The Jews will have had good reason to hate Paul; whether the Nabateans had reasons of their own or just agreed to work with the Jews is uncertain.

Although there are some unanswered questions here, the broad picture is clear enough, and there is no reason to doubt the general impression given by Acts or Paul.

4   Antioch: capital city of the East

Paul's life was becoming that of a fugitive: escaping from Damascus in a basket, then being hustled out of Jerusalem. He went to Tarsus, according to Acts, and then some time later to Antioch (9.30; 11.26). Galatians agrees with this (1.21). Actually it says that he went to Syria (whose capital was Antioch) and to Cilicia (where Tarsus was), which could mean that he went to Tarsus via Syria. But more likely Paul mentions Syria first because it is what happened there, in Antioch, that is going to be the focus of his attention (in Galatians 2).

It makes sense that Paul should return to Tarsus. He could hope to find some refuge in his home town. It was also a place where he might have wanted to go and share his new faith in the Messiah, Jesus. How welcome he will have been is another question; presumably some of his friends and family will have been very angry at his change of religious direction. We have no definite information about what he did when he got to Tarsus. He may have kept a very low profile. But it is hard to imagine him going home and not seeking to share his new faith in the synagogue circles where he grew up. Acts 15.41 speaks of Paul strengthening the churches of Syria and Cilicia, which may suggest that he did establish a church or churches in the Tarsus area. We don't know whether he developed a mission to Gentiles or how long he stayed there. Maybe it was not very long.

What we do know is that he moved on to Antioch in Syria. Acts tells us this directly (11.25, 26), and Galatians suggests the same (1.21, 2.11).

Syrian Antioch – to be distinguished from Pisidian Antioch in central Turkey – is modern Antakya, and was a very important city in New Testament times. It was the capital of the Roman province of Syria, and effectively the capital of the eastern part of the Roman Empire. It was variously described as 'the third city of the empire', 'the queen of the East', and 'Antioch the beautiful'. The senior

Roman governor of the region was based there, and a large contingent of the Roman army. It was a key city for trade, on routes from East to West, and one of the largest cities in the Roman Empire. Its population may have been as much as half a million, and it had a large and well-established Jewish community, probably of more than 20,000.

Given that it was only about 300 miles on a direct route north of Jerusalem, it seems likely that Christianity reached Antioch early. Acts says that the scattering of Christians which followed Stephen's martyrdom brought some to Antioch (11.19), and it is tempting to speculate that they may have included Nicolas, one of Stephen's colleagues in the seven, since he is said to have been a Jewish proselyte from Antioch (6.5). Acts says that they brought the message only to Jews first, but that then 'men from Cyprus and Cyrene went to Antioch and began to speak to Greeks also, telling them the good news about the Lord Jesus . . . and a great number of people believed' (11.20, 21).

Acts suggests that individual Gentiles had become Christians before, notably the family of Cornelius (Acts 10), and it is possible that Paul may have had a ministry among Gentiles in Tarsus, if not Arabia. But the impression we get from both Acts and Galatians is that Antioch was the place where Gentile Christianity really took off. It does not seem to have been recognized policy up until that time for Christians to target Gentiles. Jesus is said to have told his disciples to go and make disciples of all nations (Matthew 28.16; Acts 1.8), but the first Christians' priority, as indeed Jesus' own priority, seems to have been the Jews of Jerusalem and Judaea (see Galatians 2.7–9; Romans 15.8; Matthew 10.5, 15.24; Acts 1.8), and it was in any case natural for those from a Jewish background to go to their fellow Jews. This probably happened in Antioch at first. But the men from Cyprus and Cyrene were probably used to mixing with Gentiles, and they broke through the spiritual 'iron curtain'. And now we see a large number of Gentiles coming into the Church.

It is not hard to imagine how perplexing this may have been to the Christian leadership in Jerusalem: what were they to make of a rapidly growing Christian community full of 'unclean' Gentiles – just up the road in the important capital city?! Acts suggests that they had found it hard to accept that Cornelius and his family could

27

be baptized without being circumcised, but Peter's vision and the descent of the Holy Spirit on to the family meant that they could not come to any other conclusion (see the story in Acts 10 and 11). But they may well have seen that as an exception to the rule. It was a very different thing to have an open door to Gentiles. Of course, they would have had no problem with Gentiles coming into the church family on Jewish terms, and indeed that may well have been how they interpreted Jesus' command to make disciples from the nations. But to have a church with a large number of uncircumcised people in it was highly controversial, and to many in Jerusalem, Jewish Christians as well as Jews, it will have looked like a betrayal of their ancestral faith and culture. (It was just the sort of thing that Saul the Pharisee had been hoping to stop happening!)

The obvious thing to do in the circumstances was to send someone up to Antioch to see what was going on and to supervise this non-apostolic mission to Gentiles. It is not hard to imagine modern parallels – the Church of England hierarchy hear of rather wild-sounding charismatic goings-on in St Agatha's and send someone down to find out what is happening and to report back! The inspired choice of the Jerusalem church was Barnabas, himself a Cypriot, but someone with very good credentials in the Jerusalem church.

He came to Antioch, and Acts reports that 'when he arrived and saw the evidence of the grace of God, he was glad and encouraged them all to remain true to the Lord with all their hearts. He was a good man, full of the Holy Spirit and faith, and a great number of people were brought to the Lord' (11.23–4). If some in Jerusalem had hoped that Barnabas was going to stop the embarrassing developments in Antioch, exactly the opposite seems to have happened. Barnabas was excited by what he saw and recognized it as a genuine work of God. The Church went from strength to strength in Antioch.

Paul comes to Antioch

Barnabas's next move was an interesting one. Acts tells us that he made a hundred-mile journey to Tarsus to get Paul, bringing him back to Antioch (11.25–6). Exactly what made Barnabas do this is impossible to say. But he had met Paul in Jerusalem not all that long before, and had been convinced of the genuineness of his conversion and call. He introduced Paul to the apostles, and he evidently believed in the young man and his potential. He may well have been impressed with his brief ministry among the Greek-speakers of Jerusalem, and regretted that he had to be shipped off to Tarsus. It is possible that he knew of the ministry Paul had started in Tarsus. Whatever the exact reasons, Barnabas saw Paul as the colleague he needed in Antioch, and brought him there. Paul thus got stuck into the leadership of this important growing Jewish–Gentile church, teaching great numbers of people.

It is interesting to reflect on how the developments in Antioch will have looked from Jerusalem. To many of the Jews in Jerusalem they must have seemed disastrous: their spiritual brothers and sisters in Antioch were becoming Christians and were compromising their Jewish allegiance by mixing with unclean Gentiles – even eating with them. Quite probably the Jewish community in Antioch was split down the middle on the issue. And then to make matters worse, the arch-traitor, former Pharisee Paul came on the scene and started a very vigorous ministry, quite possibly converting more Jews to his way of thinking.

It is hard to imagine his ministry failing to agitate the local Jews, and it is interesting to speculate as to whether there may have been violent clashes between Jews and Christians; Acts suggests that this was a rather normal pattern later in Paul's ministry (Acts 13.45, 50, 14.2, etc.). There is no direct evidence of such trouble in Antioch at this time, but Acts tells us that 'the disciples were first called Christians at Antioch' (11.26); this may have been a disparaging nickname given to the Christians by their opponents, or a name used by the authorities to distinguish them from Jews. In either case it could reflect tensions between the old and the new religion.

Whether or not there was actual violence, the reports the Jews in Jerusalem were receiving from Antioch will probably have made them even more hostile than they already were towards the Christians in their own city. It may be no accident that the very next chapter of Acts refers to James the apostle being executed and Peter being arrested – by King Herod. This Herod is Herod Agrippa I, who ruled briefly in Jerusalem from AD 41–4. Acts says that he

29

made this major attack on the top leadership of the Christian church because 'this pleased the Jews' (12.1–4). What lay behind Herod's action? It seems entirely possible that Acts 11 lay behind Acts 12! In other words, the things that were going on in the Antioch church under the leadership of Barnabas and Paul were probably incensing the Jews of Jerusalem, and so the persecution of Christians in Jerusalem, which had subsided after Paul's conversion, flared up again with the appointment of Herod.

Peter escaped miraculously from Herod and went away from Jerusalem to 'another place' (12.17). It looks as though at this point Peter effectively hands over resident leadership of the Jerusalem church to James, Jesus' brother (12.17; cf. Acts 15.13; Galatians 2.12). What is interesting is that James seems to have been a rather conservative Jewish Christian, whether by conviction or necessity or both (Galatians 2.12; Acts 21.17–25; Eusebius, *Ecclesiastical History* II.23). It is not hard to see that it may have been advantageous to have someone with impeccable Jewish credentials as the leader of the church in Jerusalem at a time when Jewish hostility towards the developing Christian mission to Gentiles and to its leaders was so strong: James was not compromised in the way that Barnabas, Paul and to a lesser degree Peter were.

How the Jewish Christians in Jerusalem felt about developments in Antioch and elsewhere we cannot be sure, but they were probably under considerable pressure, as we have suggested. And for that and other reasons they may have been quite unhappy with what was going on: they may have been uneasy about the 'compromises' that their Jewish Christian brothers and sisters were making – mixing with Gentiles, etc. They will have wished that the Gentile Christians could be properly circumcised, which would have made their life much easier. They will have had particular questions about Paul's involvement in the situation: they were probably quite unhappy about their former persecutor taking a leading role in the Antioch church, and no doubt defending the liberal policy they were adopting. Barnabas after all was an authorized delegate; Paul was nothing of the sort.

It is in this general context that Acts describes the Christians of Antioch sending financial or material help to their brothers and sisters in Jerusalem. Acts says that this was in response to a prophecy of severe worldwide famine by a man called Agabus (11.27–30). But Agabus was, according to Acts, one of a group of prophets who had come recently from Jerusalem to Antioch; he and his colleagues must have brought news of the church in Jerusalem. The news they brought was, very likely, that the Christians in Jerusalem were having a difficult time and were under pressure, so that they would be particularly vulnerable to the coming famine. The Christians in Antioch will have been inspired by this news to send help to Jerusalem, all the more so if they learned that the church there was suffering because of what they were doing in Antioch. It was an act of friendship to the mother church from a troublesome child that was growing fast. To describe it as a 'peace offering' may not be exactly accurate, but it is notable that the gift was taken by Barnabas and Paul. It was a top-level delegation.

Almost everything that we have described in this chapter is based on the book of Acts, but we know that some scholars are doubtful about Acts' historical reliability. However, Paul's letter to the Galatians confirms various points. It confirms that

- Paul was in Cilicia and Syria (1.21);
- he was in Antioch (2.11);
- Paul and Barnabas were colleagues (2.1, 13);
- the Christians of Jerusalem were hard-pressed materially (2.10);
- Jewish Christians in Antioch ate with Gentiles and this was highly offensive to people in Jerusalem (2.11);
- James, Jesus' brother, had a leading role in the Jerusalem church and was associated there with a conservative Jewish Christianity (2.9, 12).

The question of Paul's second visit to Jerusalem

Although Galatians confirms various of the details, it does not, on the other hand, refer to Paul and Barnabas bringing relief from Antioch to the Jerusalem church. Instead it refers to a visit of Paul and Barnabas in which Paul explained 'the gospel that I preach among the Gentiles' to those who 'seemed to be leaders' (2.2). Paul evidently felt it necessary to defend himself. This may have been because of the 'false brethren' whom he then mentions, who evidently objected to Paul's gospel of freedom for Gentiles and argued that the Gentiles should be circumcised (2.3–5). The upshot of the discussions, as Paul describes it, was the recognition of his message and ministry by the leaders in Jerusalem: 'they saw that I had been given the task of preaching the gospel to the Gentiles, just as Peter had been given the task of preaching the gospel to the Jews' (2.7). James (Jesus' brother, named first here), Peter and John 'gave me and Barnabas the right hand of fellowship . . . they agreed that we should go to the Gentiles, and they to the Jews' (2.9). Paul refers to James, Peter and John as 'those who seemed to be important' and as 'those reputed to be pillars' (2.6, 9): this may sound a little grudging in tone, but it should be remembered that in Galatians Paul is responding to people who were putting him down as a second-class Christian leader and apostle.

The case for identifying Galatians 2.1–10 with Acts 15

This description in Galatians of the visit of Paul and Barnabas to Jerusalem does not at first sight seem very like the 'famine relief visit' of Acts 11.27–30, and many scholars have argued that it sounds much more like the great council in Jerusalem described in Acts 15. Thus in Acts 15:

- Paul and Barnabas come down from Antioch to Jerusalem;
- the issue is whether the Gentiles need to be circumcised, some people from Jerusalem arguing this very forcefully;
- the issue is talked through by Paul, Barnabas, Peter and James;
- the upshot is a decree affirming the position of Paul and Barnabas on circumcision, though requiring the Gentiles to observe some Jewish customs (e.g. dietary practices) for the sake of the Jews.

It is easy to see the attraction of identifying this account with Paul's account in Galatians 2. But there are major difficulties with the identification. One problem is that Acts 15 depicts a very public meeting, ending in official decrees that are then despatched. Galatians 2, on the other hand, suggests a private discussion of Paul and Barnabas with the 'pillars', ending with a handshake; no decrees are mentioned, nor any dietary restrictions on Gentiles.

Another problem is that the visit to Jerusalem described in Acts 15 is Paul's third visit to the Holy City after his conversion, according to Acts, the second being the famine relief visit described in chapter 11; but the visit in Galatians 2 is his second post-conversion visit.

Explaining these discrepancies is not easy. It is not very likely that Paul in Galatians 2 has forgotten the famine relief visit or just passed over it, since he is being very deliberate in detailing the limited extent of his contact with Jerusalem. The much more popular explanation is that Acts is historically confused about the visits, the famine relief visit of Acts 11 really coming later, and/or Acts 15 mixing up the private discussions of Galatians 2 with some other separate occasion on which the decrees were promulgated.

The case for identifying Galatians 2.1–10 with Acts 11.27–30

However, it is very much simpler to reject the identification of Galatians 2 with Acts 15, and to assume that the famine relief visit of Acts 11 was the visit on which Barnabas and Paul held their discussion with the 'pillars' as described in Galatians 2. In favour of this are the considerations given below.

1. Although Acts 11 does not describe Paul and Barnabas discussing the Gentile mission that had been going on in Antioch with anyone in Jerusalem, there is absolutely no way that Paul and Barnabas could have gone from Antioch to Jerusalem, as described by Acts 11, without discussing what had been happening. Even if some of our suggestions about the impact of events in Antioch on Jerusalem are speculative, it is just silly to read Acts 11 and to imagine that Paul and Barnabas would have delivered the famine relief to the elders of the church, without also having talked seriously to the top Christians in Jerusalem about the Antioch mission and in particular about Paul's controversial part in it.

2. It is true that Acts does not describe the discussions, but (*a*) Galatians suggests they were private, and (*b*) it is no surprise that the author of Luke–Acts, who is very interested in Christians giving up and sharing their money, should have focused on that aspect of the visit (cf. Luke 12.33; Acts 4.32–7).

3. It is true also that Galatians 2 does not mention the famine

relief that had been brought. But the account of Paul and Barnabas's visit ends with the comment that 'the pillars' 'asked ... that we should continue to remember the poor, the very thing I was eager to do' (2.10). This confirms that the context was one of material poverty for the Christians in Jerusalem. Furthermore, Galatians 2 says that Paul and Barnabas came up to Jerusalem 'by revelation', which might be an allusion to the prophecy of Agabus that Acts refers to (Galatians 2.1; Acts 11.28).

4. Galatians 2 suggests that perhaps the main issue at stake in the discussions was Paul's apostleship and ministry, which is exactly what we might have expected in the Acts 11 context. (The broader question of the Gentiles and what was to be required of them may not have been central on this occasion, but have come to the fore again later. Galatians 2.3–5 may refer to this later occasion.)

5. Galatians 2 has the 'pillars' give their blessing to Paul and Barnabas, 'that we should go to the Gentiles, and they to the Jews' (2.9). This fits in perfectly with the sequence of events in Acts 13, where Paul and Barnabas, having returned from the meeting in Jerusalem to Antioch, are then sent out from Antioch on what has been known as their 'first missionary journey' (vv. 2–4ff.). It is as though they are given the green light in Jerusalem to go to the Gentiles, and that is precisely what they do.

   It is interesting to notice the wording in Acts 13.2, where the Church decides to send their two leaders out: they are led to do this by the Holy Spirit, who says, 'Set apart for me Barnabas and Saul *for the work to which I have called them*'. We are not told what the 'work' is, but we could well have here an allusion back to the commission they were given in Jerusalem to 'go to the Gentiles' (Galatians 2.7, 9). The Holy Spirit now tells them to move ahead with that work which has been entrusted to them; so they do.

6. Galatians 2 makes it clear that the Jerusalem meeting with the 'pillars' did not end the controversy regarding Jewish Christians and Gentile Christians, and that in particular the question of table fellowship reared its head later when Peter

was in Antioch (2.11–23). It makes good sense to think that it was that controversy which led up to the council of Acts 15, where the decrees specifically include the request that Gentile Christians respect some Jewish dietary rules – for the sake of good relations between Gentile Christians and Jews. It fits better to have Acts 15 coming after Galatians 2 than to identify Acts 15 and the meeting of Galatians 2.1–10. (We shall come back to this point in Chapter 5.)

We conclude that Acts and Galatians both have it right: Paul's second visit to Jerusalem after his conversion was the famine relief visit of Acts 11 and 12 and that was the same visit as is described in Galatians 2. What had been going on in Antioch had been making life difficult for the Christians in Jerusalem, and in that context the bringing of material aid to Jerusalem was a very positive act of Christian friendship. But it was highly desirable also to talk the situation through, which is precisely what Paul and Barnabas did with the 'pillars'. Scholars have often failed to see this simple logic and linkage, not having appreciated the big picture suggested by Acts and Galatians.

What about dates?

Paul may well have been converted as early as AD 31 or 32. In Galatians he speaks of going to Jerusalem 'three years' after that (1.18), which would take us to AD 33–35 (depending on whether three years is three whole years, or three years counted inclusively, as may be more likely). He then says that he came up to Jerusalem 'fourteen years later', which could mean fourteen years after the earlier visit, or fourteen years after his conversion (2.1). If the former, then we are talking about a date between AD 46 and 49; if the latter, then between AD 44 and 46.

So far as the evidence of Acts is concerned, the narrative link between the famine relief visit and the account of Herod Agrippa's attack on the Church mean that a date around AD 44 or 45 would fit well (11.27–30, 12.25), but Luke leaves the exact connection quite vague ('about this time' 12.1). It would certainly make sense if Herod's attack on the church came before the famine relief visit, that visit happening shortly after Herod's death (in AD 44), when the

Christians of Jerusalem needed support, but when Peter was back in Jerusalem – though he was perhaps keeping out of sight and Paul's meeting with him and the others was 'in private' (Acts 12.23–5; Galatians 2.2). We know of severe famine in Jerusalem from AD 44–6, which would fit in with the sort of date suggested.

NOTE ON CALIGULA'S STATUE

In AD 39 or 40 the Roman emperor, Gaius Caligula, became infuriated with the Jews of Palestine and ordered that his statue be erected in the Jerusalem temple. The man who was supposed to implement the order was the newly appointed Roman governor of Syria, Petronius. But he was besieged by delegations of Jews begging him not to take this disastrous action. Fortunately the megalomaniac emperor was assassinated in Rome, and the matter was dropped. If the Christian church was established in Antioch by this time, it is interesting to speculate on the likely impact of these events on relations between Jews and Christians in Antioch. Would it have drawn them together, or would it have done the opposite, especially if the Christians were echoing Jesus' teaching and saying that the temple was going to be defiled and destroyed? If the Christian church was established after the crisis, its attitude to the temple could still constitute a particular point of tension between Christians and Jews, given the recent events. (See further Chapters 7 and 10.)

PART 2
MISSIONARY JOURNEYS AND LETTERS

5 Travels in and around Galatia

What happened next according to Acts?

After their important conciliatory visit to Jerusalem, Acts tells us that Paul and Barnabas began their travelling mission around the Mediterranean world. To be more exact, they returned to Antioch, and it was when the church there was worshipping and fasting that God said through the Holy Spirit, 'Set apart for me Barnabas and Saul for the work to which I have called them' (Acts 13.2).

There are two interesting things to be noticed here. First, this sending out, like the previous sending of them to Jerusalem with famine relief, was is in response to a prophecy. We are dealing with a church where prophecy under the inspiration of the Holy Spirit seems to have been very important. But second, if we are right about the Galatians 2 background, this prophecy did not come out of the blue; as we have seen, it may be said to have picked up on the commission that Paul and Barnabas had been given in Jerusalem to 'go to the Gentiles'. Just as the earlier prophecy of Agabus may have confirmed something that they felt was important – that a delegation should go to Jerusalem – so here it is as though the Holy Spirit, who had sorted things out in Jerusalem, was now guiding them to implement what had been agreed.

So from Antioch, capital city of the east of the Roman Empire, the city where the first strong Gentile church was established, the missionaries ('apostles' means missionaries) to the Gentiles went out, with the blessing and support of the church.

They went first to the island of Cyprus, prompted no doubt by the Holy Spirit, but it was also a very logical place for them to go, since Barnabas was a Cypriot and the Antioch church had other links with Cyprus (Acts 4.36, 11.20). Acts describes the two missionaries travelling through the whole island, and making at least one convert, who is no less than one Sergius Paulus, the proconsul (prime minister, we might say) of the island (13.12).

From Cyprus they sailed north across the Mediterranean Sea to southern Turkey (as we call it today), again a logical enough move, given that Paul came from Tarsus. They actually landed a few hundred miles west of Tarsus at Perga (Acts 13.13). The book of Acts tells us that their young companion John Mark left them at that point. It later appears that this was a matter of considerable tension between Paul and Barnabas (15.36–40). We may guess that Paul saw it as a desertion and as evidence of John Mark's lack of courage or commitment; Barnabas the encourager was more charitable, Mark being in any case his cousin (Colossians 4.10). It is just possible that Mark's loss of nerve, if that was what it was, had something to do with illness hitting the group, since in Galatians 4.13 Paul speaks of coming to the Galatians ill. Perga, where they landed, was hot, steamy and malaria-ridden, and it may be that Paul and others got ill, which led Mark to leave the party and Paul and Barnabas to head inland to the much healthier Pisidian Antioch, 1,000 metres above sea level, though it will have been an arduous 160-mile journey over the Taurus Mountains in order to get there. It is possible that Paul and Barnabas went to Pisidian Antioch at the suggestion of Sergius Paulus, since there is evidence that he had family connections with the area.

Acts in any case describes a period of fruitful ministry for Paul and Barnabas in Antioch and the neighbouring cities of Iconium, Lystra and Derbe. At Antioch and Iconium they started their ministry in the synagogue. Acts 13 describes Paul's preaching to the Jews: Paul summarizes the history of the people of Israel (in a manner reminiscent of Stephen); he then speaks of Jesus as the Messiah and as the one looked forward to by John the Baptist. He then speaks of the death of Jesus, and particularly of his resurrection, bringing in Old Testament texts. Finally he calls for the people to repent. The result of the mission was, on the one hand, the conversion of many Jews and 'God-fearers', i.e. Gentiles associated with the synagogue, and, on the other, hostility and opposition from the unbelieving Jews. This led Paul and Barnabas to turn to the Gentiles, 'for this is what the Lord has commanded us: "I have made you a light for the Gentiles, that you may bring salvation to the ends of the earth"' (13.47). The upshot of this was further conversions, but also further and increasingly violent opposition from the Jews, which finally led to their expulsion from the region.

They moved on to Iconium, a hundred miles or so to the east, where much the same pattern of events seems to have occurred, ending with plots instigated by the Jews against their lives (14.1–5). Acts refers to many miracles being done in Iconium, and when they arrived at their next destination, Lystra, the miraculous healing of a lame man led initially to great excitement among the crowd, who associated Barnabas and Paul with the gods Zeus and Hermes who, according to legend, had visited the area. But this enthusiasm later turned to vicious hostility and Paul was stoned and left for dead (14.6–20). He and Barnabas went on to Derbe, where according to Acts they won a large number of disciples (14.20, 21). At this point they turned back and retraced their steps, encouraging the churches they had established in Lystra, Iconium and Antioch to endure 'many hardships' and appointing elders in each church to lead them. They then returned to the coast and to Perga, where this time Acts says that 'they preached the word', perhaps having been unable to do so before because of illness. Then it was back to Syrian Antioch, where they stayed 'a long time with the disciples' (14.22–8).

The next thing that Acts describes is 'some men' coming down from Judaea to Antioch and 'teaching the brothers: "Unless you are circumcised, according to the custom taught by Moses, you cannot be saved."' Acts comments that 'this brought Paul and Barnabas into sharp dispute and debate with them', and led to Paul, Barnabas and others going up to Jerusalem to consult with the apostles and elders (15.1–3).

What happened next according to Paul?

We have followed the Acts account of events following Paul's second visit to Jerusalem; but is there any confirmation of the account from Paul himself? We might give a general yes to that question on the basis of Paul's second letter to the Corinthians, where Paul vividly describes some of the hardships he has experienced, contrasting his own experiences with those of his critics:

> Are they servants of Christ? (I am out of my mind to talk like this.) I am more. I have worked much harder, been in prison more frequently, been flogged more severely and been exposed to

death again and again. Five times I received from the Jews the forty lashes minus one. Three times I was beaten with rods, once I was stoned, three times I was shipwrecked, I spent a night and a day in the open sea, I have been constantly on the move. I have been in danger from rivers, in danger from bandits, in danger from my own countrymen, in danger from Gentiles; in danger in the city, in danger in the country, in danger at sea; and in danger from false brothers. I have laboured and toiled and have often gone without sleep; I have known hunger and thirst and have often gone without food; I have been cold and naked. (2 Corinthians 11.23–7)

It is a quite remarkable catalogue of hardships, and in various ways it fits in with the Acts account of Paul's missionary journey with Barnabas that we have been examining. In particular it mentions stoning on one occasion; but there is also the reference to receiving the 'forty lashes minus one'. This was a Jewish penalty, forty being the maximum number of lashes allowed under Old Testament law; 'minus one' was to make sure that the limit was not exceeded (cf. Deuteronomy 25.3). The fact that Paul suffered this penalty five times confirms that he was in close contact with the synagogues and came into conflict with them, as Acts also tells us.

Some people have questioned Acts on precisely this point, observing that Paul saw his mission as to the Gentiles, not to the Jews, and finding a conflict between this and the impression given in Acts that Paul regularly started his missionary visits in the synagogue. However, it is perfectly clear, and not just from the 2 Corinthians passage quoted above, that Paul did not see his commission as barring him from contact with Jews or the synagogue (see also 1 Corinthians 9.20). He saw his mission as going 'to the nations', but he believed also that the gospel was 'first for the Jew' (Romans 1.16), and his natural point of entry to the Gentile cities he visited was via the Jewish community. It is worth remembering that synagogues typically had a number of Gentile 'God-fearers', so that ministering in the synagogue was a way of reaching sympathetic Gentiles as well as Jews (Acts 17.4, 17).

The 2 Corinthians 11 passage also has references to dangerous travel, which fit the picture given by Acts. When we read of Paul journeying from place to place in Acts most of us have little concept of what those journeys were like; but if we were to trace Paul's route on the ground, we would realise what huge distances he travelled (hundreds of miles – on foot), how rough and lonely some of the terrain was (for example over the Taurus Mountains in southern Turkey, which rise to almost 4,000 metres), and how exhausting and dangerous it must have been both on the dirt roads, with bandits a constant worry, and also on the sea in small sailing boats.

But although 2 Corinthians 11 fits in with Acts' description of Paul's 'first missionary journey', it is a general description covering not just that journey, but other subsequent and/or earlier ones. Does Galatians help us more specifically with the events of this period? We have seen how Paul tells the Galatians in some detail what happened leading up to that historic visit to Jerusalem when Paul and Barnabas were given the green light to go to the Gentiles. Unfortunately it is not so clear what happened after that. However, various things have happened by the time Galatians was written.

1. Paul has been to Galatia, been warmly welcomed by many of the Galatians, and has founded churches there – hence his letter.
2. Paul has heard alarming news about false brothers, as he sees them, coming into the Galatian church and persuading them that they need to be circumcised and to keep the Jewish law (1.7–9, 6.12 and *passim*).
3. There has been a difficult dispute in Antioch involving Paul, Peter and Barnabas, and 'certain men from James' (2.11–21). The dispute was over the matter of Jewish Christians eating with Gentile Christians. Peter had come to Antioch and at the beginning had eaten meals with the Gentiles, along with Paul, Barnabas and everyone. But then the 'men from James' came, and Peter began to withdraw and separate himself, 'because he was afraid of those who belonged to the circumcision group'. Other Jewish Christians did the same, including, to Paul's horror, Barnabas, his senior colleague and earlier leader of the largely Gentile church in Antioch (2.12, 13).

There are lots of interesting questions raised by these observations. For example, when did the Antioch dispute take place? It seems unlikely that it took place immediately after the agreement with the 'pillars' in Jerusalem, when they sorted things out together. It seems likely that it took place after Barnabas and Paul had been on their evangelistic journey to Galatia and perhaps just before Paul wrote Galatians: if it was old history before the time of his mission to Galatia, why would he tell them about the embarrassing incident? If it was very recent history and even part of the same thing that was going on in Galatia (i.e. a campaign by the circumcision party to have Paul's position overturned), then Paul's very agitated and heated remarks are explicable, and so is his failure to say what happened after the dispute. Some scholars have speculated that Paul lost out in the dispute, hence his failure to mention the outcome. But if so, why would he have mentioned it to the Galatians? It seems much more likely that the situation was an ongoing and unresolved one – in Galatia and Antioch.

Relating Acts and Galatians

But how might this relate to Acts? One of the much debated questions is: where is Galatia? The Galatians came originally from central Europe in the Danube region, some migrating to Gaul (i.e. France) and some to Asia Minor, i.e. Turkey, to the region of Ancyra (modern Ankara). Paul could have been writing to those ethnic Galatians. However, the Roman province of Galatia spread almost 200 miles south of Ancyra and included the ethnically different areas of Pisidia and Lycaonia, where the cities of Antioch, Iconium, Lystra and Derbe were located. So when Paul wrote to the Galatians, was he writing to the ethnic Galatians (the North Galatian theory) or to the provincial Galatians of places like Pisidian Antioch (the South Galatian theory)? The South Galatian theory is much more likely, despite some scholars who think otherwise. Paul quite regularly uses provincial names for areas he has worked in (e.g. 1 Corinthians 16.1, 5, 15, 19; 2 Corinthians 9.2; Romans 15.26), and it would have been the obvious way to refer to the different towns of South Galatia. And, although it is possible to speculate that Acts 16.6 and 18.23 could refer to a ministry in North Galatia, Acts gives ample and much less disputable evidence of a significant and successful ministry in South Galatia.

But more important than these arguments is the way that the Acts and Galatians accounts dovetail. On this view:

1. Acts 11 and 12 and Galatians 2.1–10 describe Paul and Barnabas going up to Jerusalem with aid for the distressed church and discussing their ministry with Peter, James and John. The outcome of the discussions was a recognition of their calling to go to the Gentiles.
2. This was followed by the Antioch church sending them out: they went first to Cyprus, then to South Galatia. They had a successful ministry there, establishing churches in several centres (Acts 13; also Galatians).
3. But their ministry caused deep divisions in the Jewish communities of the area, and antagonism that turned violent. Inevitably news of this will have reached the Jewish leaders in Jerusalem. Inevitably also this will have put the Jewish Christians in Jerusalem under renewed pressure from the Jewish authorities and others; the Christians may very well have felt that they were fighting for their lives. So some of these Jewish Christians from Jerusalem went out to various places to try and bring the 'liberal' converts of Paul and Barnabas into line. Some went to Galatia, some to Antioch.
4. Paul and Barnabas returned to Antioch. At some point Peter had also come there. At first he accepted the practice of the church, which was that Gentile and Jewish Christians ate meals together, as part of their worship. It is not surprising that he did so, if Acts is right to say that he had an amazing vision from God telling him to go to the Gentile centurion Cornelius and that he had then seen God pour out his Holy Spirit on that uncircumcised family (Acts 10). What may seem much more surprising is that the Christians in Jerusalem, having heard of that event, could later have had doubts about uncircumcised Gentiles. Even more surprising is that Peter could have been persuaded to withdraw from eating with Gentiles. Does this cast doubt on the whole story of Cornelius? Not necessarily. Paul's whole point in his description of the incident is that Peter's withdrawal was an extraordinary change of policy; even more amazing was Barnabas's joining

Peter in this, since Barnabas had for so long been part of the open approach to Gentiles. Now even he withdrew. Why? Clearly some very cogent arguments were being pressed by the men claiming to come from James.

It seems unlikely that Barnabas or Peter were acceding to the view that Gentiles needed to be circumcised. What seems quite likely are the points given below.

1. The issue was one of Jewish Christians defiling themselves by eating unclean food. What the Gentiles were doing was not a major worry to orthodox Jews; what was really upsetting was their fellow Jews giving up their commitment to the law and traditions of the fathers, and defiling themselves, for example by eating unclean food with Gentiles. (See Acts 21.21 for the later charge against Paul 'that you teach all the Jews who live among the Gentiles to turn away from Moses, telling them not to circumcise their children or live according to our customs'.)

2. The Jewish Christians were under acute pressure from the Jews in Jerusalem on this very point. We know from the Jewish historian Josephus that Jewish nationalism was militant in this period, various insurgency movements being forcibly suppressed by the Roman authorities; it is likely that the Christians in Jerusalem will have been under attack from their fellow Jews, because of their supposed liberalism towards the law and their fraternizing with Gentiles. Paul comments in Galatians 6.12 that the so-called Judaizers were doing what they were only 'to avoid being persecuted for the cross of Christ'. Paul's accusation could be without any basis, but it could be exactly right: the Jewish Christians were not just finding it difficult to witness in Jerusalem, but were being actively vilified and attacked.

3. A particular cause of friction, as we have suggested already, was the mission of Paul and Barnabas in Galatia, where they had divided the Jewish community – disastrously from a Jewish point of view. Things will have been made all the worse by reports arriving from Antioch that Peter, the Christians' leader, was defiling himself. It is possible to imagine Peter being warned by the Jewish Christians who

came to Antioch that he was forfeiting all respect as leader of the Church by his conduct; it is possible to imagine them recalling that his commission was particularly to go 'to the circumcised' (Galatians 2.7, 8), and it is possible to imagine him and Barnabas too responding to the crisis that their brothers and sisters were experiencing in Jerusalem by withdrawing from table fellowship with Gentiles.

It seems improbable, as we have said, that Peter and Barnabas thought they were compelling the Gentiles to be circumcised by their action. They may have seen it as a temporary measure, or indeed they may have been moving unconsciously towards denominationalism – with separate Lord's tables for Jewish and Gentile Christians. But for Paul with his sharp logical mind, it was a betrayal of the Gentiles not to eat with them, and it was in effect saying that you do need to be circumcised in order to be a full member of the people of God. Paul saw it as theologically fatal (so 2.14–21).

It is easy to see how the arguments could have been heated and sharp. Both Paul and Peter were motivated by missionary concern – Paul for Gentile mission, Peter and Barnabas for Jewish mission in Jerusalem. Acts 15.2 also speaks of 'no little dissension and debate'. Galatians was probably written in this context, hence Paul's pained tone and the fact that he mentions no resolution to the conflict. Hence also his writing the letter in the first person and not mentioning Barnabas's work among the Galatians (though he assumes that they know him, and that he and Barnabas were a team); at the time of writing the letter relations between Barnabas and Paul were very strained. (It is also interesting to notice how in Acts Paul seems to take the lead in the Galatian mission, Barnabas becoming less prominent – e.g. note the change from 'Barnabas and Saul' to 'Paul and Barnabas' in chapter 13, also 14.12.)

The result of all this was the so-called Council of Jerusalem, described in Acts 15. The contributors to the discussion were, as we would now expect, the circumcision party, Paul, Barnabas, Peter and James. And the resulting decision reflects precisely the issues that were at stake: first, whether the Gentiles should be circumcised and required to keep all the Jewish law; and second, how offence to the Jews could be avoided and table fellowship between Christians be maintained. The answer to the first was a clear no, thus vindicating Paul; the answer to the second was that the Gentile Christians would be asked to avoid various major causes of offence to the Jews: 'you are to abstain from food sacrificed to idols, from blood, from the meat of strangled animals, and from sexual immorality' (Acts 15.29).

It could be said that this decision represented a compromise between Paul and Peter, but it would be better to see it as a principled decision that covers both of their concerns, since it equivocally endorsed Paul's insistence that Christians are free from the law, but also insisted that Christians should not cause unnecessary offence to others (something that Paul himself strongly advocates, e.g. in 1 Corinthians 9.12–23). It also recognized Peter's concern for Jewish Christians and for Jews – for whom Moses was read every sabbath in the synagogues (15.21). It also once again made possible table fellowship between Jewish Christians and Gentile Christians, which both Paul and Peter favoured.

One conclusion of this discussion is that the accounts of Acts and Galatians fit very well together indeed, just as one might expect from two different but reliable witnesses. Another conclusion is that Galatians is the earliest of Paul's New Testament letters, having been written just at the time of the Antioch incident. A probable date is approximately AD 48. Some scholars have noticed how similar Galatians is to Romans in the themes and ideas that it propounds, and so have argued that Galatians must be dated nearer to the date of Romans, i.e. about AD 57. But this is a fallacious argument. In the first place, Galatians and Romans are quite different in tone, Galatians being anxious, almost strident, but Romans much more measured. And secondly, Galatians and Romans are thematically similar, because the same issue of Jewish and Gentile Christians kept recurring: when Paul wrote Romans he was heading for Jerusalem and he knew that he was going to confront the issues once again (15.31; see also Acts 21). So the recurrence of similar ideas and arguments is only to be expected.

6 What is going on in Galatians?

Galatians is a red-hot letter, written with great passion and force. Having travelled in the previous chapter with Paul through Galatia and having tried to reconstruct the historical sequence of events from Acts and from Paul's letters, we now turn specifically to Galatians, to see what we can learn from the letter about Paul and his ministry. In the following chapter we will consider what we can deduce about his relationship with Jesus.

Paul's context and Paul's opponents

One of the intriguing questions when reading any of Paul's letters is: what led to the writing of this letter? Most of the letters are responses to particular situations, but it is not always easy to work out what those situations were. Scholars speak of a process of 'mirror-reading': we look into the letters, and try to see what situations are reflected – whom Paul is speaking to or about. Others have said that it is like hearing one end of a phone conversation and trying to work out what the person at the other end is saying. It is not always an easy task, especially if the person on 'this end' is agitated.

However, we have already had plenty of clues about what was happening in Galatia, and some things are very clear from Paul's letter to the Galatians. Thus Paul usually begins his letters by giving thanks for people; he does this even with the wayward Corinthians (1 Corinthians 1.4). But with the Galatians there is no opening thanksgiving; instead Paul jumps straight in with a pained comment: 'I am astonished that you are so quickly deserting the one who called you by the grace of Christ and are turning to a different gospel – which is really no gospel at all. Evidently, some people are throwing you into confusion and are trying to pervert the gospel of Christ' (1.6). Here is clear evidence that the Galatians are being led away from what Paul taught them – and soon after his visit – by people wanting to correct Paul's teaching. Paul goes on to say that he wishes those who distort the good news to be accursed (1.8, 9).

49

The conclusion of the letter is equally informative. Paul takes up the pen from his scribe to whom he has been dictating, and writes: 'See what large letters I use as I write to you with my own hand' (6.11). He then goes on very bluntly: 'Those who want to make a good impression outwardly are trying to compel you to be circumcised. The only reason they do this is to avoid being persecuted for the cross of Christ. Not even those who are circumcised obey the law, yet they want you to be circumcised that they may boast about your flesh' (6.12–13). The issue is Gentile Christians being circumcised: Paul saw it as unnecessary for salvation; the people who had come after him were pressing it on the Galatians.

The contents of the letter between that beginning and that ending suggest more about how Paul's opponents argued their case:

1. They were critical of Paul, accusing him of being a manpleaser (by not insisting on circumcision), arguing that his version of the gospel was his human idea; they suggested that he was a second-class Christian leader, who hadn't been commissioned or taught by Jesus but who had been dependent on the true apostles (1.11–17). It is important to realize that Paul's opponents weren't abandoning their Christian faith, but were accusing Paul of teaching a corrupted, watered-down version of the way of Jesus.

2. They appealed to the Old Testament, in particular referring to Abraham and to circumcision as the sign given to Abraham of his special relationship with God and as a mark of the people of God. If the Galatians were to be members of the people of God and children of Abraham, then circumcision was for them too. Jesus hadn't changed that. As for the law of Moses, Paul's opponents no doubt insisted that it was given by God to his people, and that it was vital guidance for ethical living. To abandon the law in the way Paul advocated was a recipe for moral anarchy, and, as they may well have argued, it was contrary to the way of Jesus, who did not advocate abandoning the law of God. (We infer that this was what they were arguing from the tenor of Paul's reply in chapters 3–5; we can imagine them citing sayings of Jesus such as Matthew 5.17–19.)

How does Paul respond to these charges?

With emotion

Paul responds not with cold logical dispassionate arguments, but with heated emotion. As we saw, he speaks of his astonishment at their rapid defection from the good news they had received (1.6). He asks, 'Who has bewitched you?' (3.1), and asks what has come of their love and devotion to him when he visited them; he compares his agonies now over what is happening with the labours of a mother giving birth (4.15–20). He is hostile towards the incomers who have undermined his work, and calls down a curse on those who preach another gospel (1.7–9). He wishes that those who unsettle the Galatians would mutilate themselves rather than circumcise others (5.12)! He claims that, though they ingratiated themselves with the Galatians, their motivation was not the welfare of the Galatians but their own good standing – presumably with the Jews – and the avoidance of persecution (6.12–13, 4.17).

By insisting on the God-given nature of his gospel

As for their arguments, we have seen that he rejects the charge that his gospel is man-made and second-hand, arguing that he had a first-hand revelation of God and derived his gospel from that, not from any human being (see Chapter 2 above). He was not heavily dependent on the Jerusalem apostles, rather the opposite. He hardly went to Jerusalem at all after his conversion, though after fourteen years he did lay his gospel before the Jerusalem apostles, and they recognized it and gave him and Barnabas the right hand of fellowship (1.10—2.10).

By emphasizing grace

As for the arguments about circumcision and the law, Paul sees the reinstatement of the law as a contradiction of the good news of Christ, with its focus on grace, the cross and faith.

The importance of 'grace' in Galatians is evident in the way Paul starts the main part of the letter by lamenting the Galatians' desertion of the one who called them '*by the grace of Christ*' (1.6). He believes that the Galatians are being misled into 'setting aside the grace of God' (2.21), and that this is fatal (see also 5.4). It is

51

probably significant that 'grace' is at the heart of Paul's greetings at the very beginning and end of the letter ('Grace and peace to you from God our Father and the Lord Jesus Christ, who gave himself for our sins to rescue us': [1.3–4]; 'The grace of our Lord Jesus Christ be with your spirit' [6.18]). Paul could simply be using standard forms of greeting here, but his use of the word 'grace' (*charis*) rather than the usual Greek 'greetings' (*chairei*) was probably deliberate. In 1.4 and also 2.21 he explains the grace of Christ in terms of Christ giving his life on the cross; so also in 2.20 he speaks of the 'Son of God who gave himself for me'. Paul does not want the Galatians to be led away from the grace and gift of God.

By focusing on the cross

Grace and the cross belong together for Paul. And the centrality of the cross for the apostle is seen, not only in the opening greeting that we have already discussed, but also at the end of the letter, when he takes the pen himself and sums things up. He contrasts the position of those who boast in things like circumcision with his own attitude: 'May I never boast except in the cross of our Lord Jesus Christ, through which the world has been crucified to me, and I to the world. Neither circumcision nor uncircumcision means anything; what counts is a new creation' (6.14–15). The cross for Paul was a world-changing, life-changing event, bringing new creation to those who have faith. He can speak of being 'crucified with Christ', so that 'I no longer live, but Christ lives in me' (2.20).

Paul believes that Jesus died for our sins – for those sins for which the law of God condemns us – taking the curse of the law on himself. He recalls the declaration in Deuteronomy, 'Cursed is everyone who is hung on a tree' (3.13), and says that Christ died to redeem or liberate us from the curse of the law 'in order that the blessing given to Abraham might come to the Gentiles through Christ Jesus, so that by faith we might receive the promise of the Spirit' (3.14). In other words the cross is God in his love sending Jesus to take our curse, to rescue us from the sinful 'world', to bring us into 'new creation', to bring us into the family of God as children of God having the Spirit of God.

So, for Paul, those who are trying to make the law an essential criterion for membership of the people of God are seriously mistaken. They are effectively denying the central importance of the cross: on their scheme, 'Christ died for nothing' (2.21). Why did he need to die, if the way to being right with God is via circumcision and the law, which we had already? Paul thinks that they are pressing their view in order to avoid 'the offence of the cross' and to save their own skins (5.11, 6.12).

By emphasizing faith

The way a person receives the grace of God which Christ won for us is by faith, another key theme in Galatians (e.g. 2.15—3.14). Faith is receiving the gift. It involves accepting God's promise, as Abraham did (3.18). For the Christian it means believing the good news of Christ, and expressing that belief in baptism. Baptism in Paul's day probably involved the candidate stepping into a pool or river, declaring his or her faith in Jesus, being wholly immersed in the water, and coming up. For Paul that dramatic moment represented the believer being crucified with Jesus, going down with him into death, and then rising to share his new life, in the family of God (see also 3.26–9).

Paul appeals to the Galatians' own experience of conversion to prove the point about faith (3.1–5), because, when they heard the story of Jesus and his death, they came to faith and received the Holy Spirit. It was a powerful experience – Paul can refer to miracles happening among them – and it clearly meant a lot to them. Paul therefore now asks them: 'did you receive the Spirit by observing the law, or by hearing the good news and putting your faith in Jesus?' The answer is clear. Why, then, do they now think that keeping the law may be necessary?

By showing that Abraham was a man of faith and Christians are his family

As for arguments from the Old Testament, Paul sees Abraham as a key figure, and as an ally in his cause. He accepts the Jewish view of him as the father of God's people, and sees Christians as becoming members of his family (3.29). But he argues from the Old Testament as follows:

- Abraham himself was right with God through faith. He quotes Genesis 15.6, where it is said: 'He believed God, and it was credited to him as righteousness.' This is a very useful text for Paul, emphasizing Abraham's faith (in the promises made to him by God), and speaking of 'righteousness' being credited to him – not earned by his good deeds or anything else (3.6). It was a covenant of grace (3.18).
- In another Genesis text God promises Abraham that 'all nations will be blessed through you' (12.3). The word 'nations' in the Greek (*ethne*) could as well be translated 'Gentiles', and so Paul sees here a promise anticipating the Gentiles being brought into Abraham's blessing.
- Yet another Genesis text has God make his promises to Abraham and his 'seed' (17.7–9). Modern English translations of Genesis use something like 'descendants' for the Hebrew word 'seed', which is indeed the natural meaning. But Paul, in a rather typically Jewish rabbinic way, sees significance in the use of the singular word, because he sees Jesus as the one who is *the* seed of Abraham, in whom God's promises to Abraham are fulfilled and through whom we may now be Abraham's 'seed' (3.16, 29). It is an argument which may seem a little strange to us, but which reflects Paul's convictions about Jesus and would have been appropriate when debating with those wanting to reimpose the Old Testament law.
- Abraham gets into Paul's argument in one other way. In chapter 4 Paul talks about Abraham's two sons, Isaac and Ishmael. Isaac was born to Sarah, Isaac's wife, by miraculous divine intervention, because Sarah was infertile and very old; Ishmael was born to Hagar, Sarah's slave girl, with whom Abraham had sex when Sarah was unable to conceive. Although Ishmael was born first, he and his mother were driven from Abraham's home, largely due to the cruel jealousy of Sarah, and went out into the desert, where they made their home and where Ishmael is said to have become the ancestor of various of the tribes who lived in the Sinai desert near Egypt (see Genesis 16 and 21). In Galatians Paul takes this famous story and does something remarkable with it: the Jews saw themselves as God's chosen people, the children of Abraham

and Isaac. Paul suggests that actually those Jews who are now insisting on the law, given on Mount Sinai, correspond to Ishmael, son of the slave woman. Christians, on the other hand, who trust in the miracle-producing promises of God, correspond to Isaac.

It is easy to see how much these arguments would have infuriated Paul's Jewish opponents, who prided themselves on being the true children of Abraham, and some of these arguments probably seem rather strange to us. But it is not difficult to see how Paul could have understood the Old Testament story as an intriguing picture of what was going on in Galatia, with the conflict between the do-it-yourself law-keeping approach of the Judaizers and his own trust-in-the-promises-and-mercy-of-God approach. Paul sees the Christians as the true spiritual family of Abraham, as the true Israel (6.16).

By explaining his perspective on the law

But what about the Old Testament law? What does Paul say to those who see that as the key to being right with God and to ethical living?

The failure of the law

Paul is quite clear, first, that the law does not make anyone right with God. In recounting his confrontation with Peter he makes this point, and quotes himself as saying to Peter: 'We who are Jews by birth and not Gentile sinners know that a person is not justified by works of the law, but by faith in Jesus Christ' (2.15). But how does Paul know this? Is it simply that he and others know positively that faith in Jesus is the way, and so conclude negatively that the law is not the way? Clearly Paul's own experience was something like that: his miraculous meeting of Jesus on the Damascus Road made clear to him the bankruptcy (or worse) of following the law and, on the other hand, the grace of God in Jesus.

However, what Paul discovered on the Damascus Road was not just that Jesus had come and so the law (which had been perfectly good) was now out of date. He discovered himself to have been a terrible sinner, persecuting the Messiah, and the law had not prevented that; indeed in one sense it had colluded in it! (This is something Paul expounds directly in Romans 7.) So the problem with the law is not just that it has been displaced, but that it didn't produce the goods, in terms of right relationship with God and right living.

It is interesting, in view of the chronological connections we have suggested, that in Acts 15 we find Peter (after his painful debate with Paul) making exactly this point to those wanting to impose the law on the Gentiles: 'Now then, why do you try to test God by putting on the necks of the disciples a yoke that neither we nor our fathers have been able to bear? No! We believe it is through the grace of our Lord Jesus that we are saved' (vv. 10–11).

That is exactly Paul's view: the law is a failure in terms of producing right relationship with God and obedient, ethical living. The fact is that we – and Paul speaks of 'we who are Jews by birth and not Gentile sinners' – are all sinners, shut up under sin (3.22). And the law did not help get us out. Paul knew that very well from his experience, and he comments that those who are pressurizing the Galatians to keep the law themselves fail to obey it (6.13).

Far from getting us out, the law pronounces a curse on us, because the Old Testament says that you need to keep the law to have life and that you are cursed if you don't (Galatians 3.10–12; Leviticus 18.5; Deuteronomy 27.26). Paul sees that as catching out not just Gentiles, but Jews, even the most law-zealous Jews such as he had been. As he says later in Romans, quoting the Old Testament: 'there is no-one righteous, not even one' (3.10).

Does that mean that Paul is – at least for the sake of argument – implying that everyone who lived before Jesus was condemned and cursed by God? Clearly it doesn't, because he knows about Abraham. He also knows about Old Testament sacrifice and about the Day of Atonement, prescribed in the Book of Moses; these important institutions show vividly that the Old Testament knows about human transgression of the law and about God forgiving transgression. Indeed it is in this context that Paul will explain the death of Jesus (most clearly in Romans 3.25). But to those who insist that keeping the law is the way to be right with God and a member of the people of God, his message is: keep it then, all of it! But that is precisely what no one is able to do (as the law, with its internal way of dealing with sin, itself attests). Depending on law-keeping is the route to a curse. And we need the route of Abraham, or rather the way of Christ.

The purpose of the law

But why then did God give the law, if we were not going to be able to keep it and if it was never intended to lead us to life? Paul's answer is that it had a temporary role 'because of transgressions' (3.19). It is interesting that he comments in that verse that the law was given through angels; this was a Jewish tradition, and perhaps at this point Paul picks up that tradition in order to demote the law a little! Of course it came from God ultimately, but it came slightly indirectly!

Paul explains the role of the law using the Greek concept of a *paidagogos* (3.19—4.10). Interestingly, the word *paidagogos* is related to our English term 'pedagogy' (i.e. the science of education), but it referred in Paul's time to the slave whom a rich family would employ to look after the children, and to keep them in order. The *paidagogos* would take them to and from school, and have a sort of disciplinary role, chastising them (literally) if they transgressed the rules. We can imagine that, although he performed a very useful role, his wards will often have chafed under the rod of this slave who was their master. And we can imagine what a sense of release there will have been when the child came of age, and was no longer under the slave, but son (or daughter) with full rights in the household.

Paul sees the law as like that slave: telling us when we have done wrong, checking and controlling us, until Jesus Christ should come. Now that he has come, Paul says that we, who were effectively in slavery under the law, are now free; we are now sons and heirs of God, with the Spirit of God in us. It makes no sense at all to want to go back to the regime of the law. Paul asks the Galatians how they can want to turn back to 'those weak and miserable principles': the Greek word here may be correctly translated 'principles' and be a reference to the demands of the law, which were weak and miserable in the sense that they did not make them good people who were right with God. But the word 'principles' could also mean 'spiritual powers', and Paul could be saying that when they were under the law, the Jews were prey to all sorts of sinful forces, luring and humiliating them. Either way, Paul suggests that it is absurd to want to go back from the experience of sonship to the regime of the *paidagogos*.

The Spirit and the law

But isn't Paul's law-free gospel a recipe for moral anarchy? Certainly it might have looked that way a few years later when the Corinthian Christians were proclaiming that 'all things are permissible', and were getting into various kinds of immorality and idolatry (see 1 Corinthians 6 and 11). The worst fears of Paul's opponents seemed to be justified. But Paul replies to claims that his gospel is morally inadequate by referring to the Holy Spirit. We have seen how the Galatians had a powerful experience of the Spirit when becoming Christians (3.1–5), and for Paul the Holy Spirit was at the heart of the Christian experience. He is the Spirit who was in Jesus (4.6), and who marks us out as children not just of Abraham, but of God himself (3.29, 4.7). This Holy Spirit of God is the one who changes us ethically. We used to live according to 'the flesh', as Paul expresses it; the word 'flesh' refers not to our physical bodies, but to our sinful human nature. But then we were crucified with Jesus, and that old fleshly life of failure, which was condemned by the law, was finished and we were raised to life in the Spirit (5.16–25). This new life is one marked by the 'fruit' of the Spirit, which Paul lists as 'love, joy, peace, patience, kindness, goodness, faithfulness, gentleness and self-control'. Paul comments, perhaps slightly amusingly, 'against such things there is no law' (5.22–4). Here indeed is the answer to those who see Paul's law-free gospel as a licence for sin; on the contrary, living by the Spirit and living therefore in love is fulfilling the law, since 'the entire law is fulfilled in a single command, "Love your neighbour as yourself"' (5.14). In saying this Paul is not advocating the modern idea that a person can be loving and sit loose to all other commandments; what he means is that the Christian who is free from the law but living by the Spirit in love will, paradoxically, fulfil the moral law of God in a way that was not possible under Judaism (compare Romans 8.4, 13.8–10).

Paul is not under the illusion that all Christians will live perfectly. He speaks of a conflict going on in the Christian between the old sinful life of the 'flesh' and the new life of the Spirit. And he calls the Galatian Christians to live out their crucifixion with Christ and their new life (5.19–25). But, although he emphasizes the importance of this, and even warns Christians that those who live the old life will not inherit the kingdom of God, still he is clear that the difference between being 'under the law' and 'in the Spirit' is the difference between slavery to sin and being a redeemed child of God equipped with the potential to live the life of the new creation.

7 What does Galatians tell us about Paul and Jesus?

We have looked at Paul's forthright teaching in Galatians and at the situation that gave rise to it. In doing so, we have touched on the history of the Galatian church and on Paul's foundational role (with Barnabas). But can we use the Galatian letter to work out further what happened when Paul founded that church, and in particular to deduce anything of what Paul originally taught the Galatians, when he and Barnabas brought the good news to them? Most or all of Paul's letters are pastoral letters to established Christian churches, and so they tell us little about Paul's evangelism. We could say that the letters are picking up the pieces afterwards, not laying the foundations! So what did Paul teach and preach when he arrived in a place like Pisidian Antioch? The purpose of this chapter is to see if we can throw light on that matter, and especially on the question as to what Paul taught people about Jesus. We saw at the beginning of the book that some scholars suggest that traditions of Jesus' ministry were not particularly important to Paul, and that he was not a very loyal follower of Jesus. Does the evidence from Acts and particularly from Galatians about Paul's early ministry support this view?

Acts gives us some brief descriptions of Paul's teaching in Galatia. In particular there is the account of his preaching in the synagogue in Pisidian Antioch, which we looked at in chapter 5. Paul traces the history of Israel through to King David, then identifies Jesus as David's son and Israel's promised saviour. He speaks of John the Baptist's announcement of Jesus and then of Jesus' death and resurrection, supporting his argument with Old Testament quotations. He closes his sermon with a challenge to his hearers to respond to the grace of God (Acts 13.16–43). Paul's emphasis when speaking to the idolatrous Gentiles in Lystra, who are trying to worship him and Barnabas, is understandably different: he speaks to them of the living God and of the need to turn from idols (Acts 14.14–17).

This evidence from Acts is interesting, but very brief. It is intriguing that Paul says to the people of Pisidian Antioch that through Jesus 'everyone who believes is justified from everything you could not be justified from by the law of Moses' (13.39); this comment about grace and law is reminiscent of Galatians. It is also interesting that Paul speaks of Jesus in the context of John the Baptist, because this reminds us of how the gospels trace the beginning of Jesus' ministry to John. Did Paul tell the story of Jesus from John through to his resurrection? We could reasonably deduce this from Acts, but was the author of Acts well informed, or was he just making Paul say what he wanted him to say? What does the evidence of Galatians suggest?

Many of the things that Paul teaches and emphasizes in Galatians – his emphasis on the living Jesus, on grace, and on the law – could directly or indirectly have come to him through his own conversion experience. Indeed he says that he got his gospel by direct revelation (1.12). But did Paul know anything about the ministry of Jesus in Palestine? And was it important to him in his ministry in Galatia?

Answering that question is rather like detective work. It is, in some ways, an even more subtle business than mirror-reading the situation and views of Paul's opponents, since we are now working at two stages removed from what we want to know:

stage 1. Paul's letter to the Galatians
stage 2. the events and ideas in Galatia which gave rise to Galatians
stage 3. the teaching of Paul when he was in Galatia, to which stage 2 was a response

It might seem like a wild goose chase trying to get back to stage 3, and likely to be pure speculation. But I am reminded of how modern crash investigators manage to deduce an enormous amount about the history of what happened by looking carefully at the debris of a train or plane crash; I suggest that we can do something analogous with Paul's letters (though they are anything but debris!).

It is important for the detective who is looking for clues in order to answer a particular question not to assume the answer and then find and interpret the evidence in line with that answer: so, a piece of concrete near a railway bridge does not prove that vandals derailed the train. Similarly an idea or phrase occurring both in Paul's letters and the gospels does not prove that Paul knew the relevant gospel story. Different possible explanations need to be considered and weighed. But, although we need to be critical and not naive, we also need to be observant and imaginative in making sense of the clues and piecing the evidence together. Readers are invited to come on the investigation!

The cross and resurrection of Jesus

The first thing that is obvious from Galatians is that Paul had taught the Galatians about the death of Jesus. It was so important for Paul himself, as we have seen, and he comments: 'Before your very eyes Jesus Christ was clearly portrayed as crucified' (3.1). It is not certain exactly what Paul means by this phraseology, but at the very least it shows that the Galatians had been taught about the cross of Jesus. He can refer to it as something that they know about.

As for what they had been taught about Jesus' death, we may be sure that Paul will have taught them that it was all to do with 'the Son of God, who loved me and gave himself for me' (2.20). But did he tell them the story of the crucifixion? He must surely have done so in some way or other. Paul speaks of 'the cross' as something he boasts about, and of crucifixion as being at the heart of Christianity; this would have made no sense at all to his hearers, for whom crucifixion was a contemporary, brutal form of execution. Paul must have told them about Jesus' death, and have explained how it could be seen as the supreme sign of God's love and as a way of salvation. The reference to Christ being 'portrayed as crucified' quite likely implies a description of the crucifixion. And it may well be that Paul's rather obscure comments about his own body bearing the marks (the *stigmata*, in Greek) of Jesus in 6.17 allude to the marks of flogging and crucifixion on Jesus; does Paul see these as mirrored in the physical wounds that he has received in his service of Christ?

One way or another, it seems entirely probable that the story of Jesus' crucifixion will have been told. Luke in his gospel includes the story of the penitent thief who was crucified with Jesus: the thief admitted his wrongdoing, and, although a sinner worthy of death, is promised a place in paradise by Jesus (Luke 23.40–2). It is a story that would have appealed to Paul – as illustrating the saving love of Jesus on the cross for sinners; it could just conceivably have contributed to his reflections on being 'crucified with Christ' (2.20). But there is no evidence of this.

Paul will also have taught the Galatians about Jesus' resurrection. He refers to it in the very first verse of Galatians, and speaks of Christ living now 'in me' (2.20). He takes it for granted that they know about it, and he does not need to explain the idea to them.

Jesus as Son of God having the Spirit

But did Paul teach them anything about Jesus' life leading up to his death and resurrection? Despite some scholars who seem to think that he might not have done so, it is highly unlikely that Paul could have preached Jesus without telling his hearers about the one who died and rose again. They would inevitably have asked who was this person who was crucified by the Romans.

The nearest Paul comes to telling us the story of Jesus in Galatians is in 4.4–6, where he says: 'When the time had fully come, God sent his Son, born of a woman, born under law, to redeem those under law, that we might receive the full rights of sons. Because you are sons, God sent the Spirit of his Son into our hearts, the Spirit who calls out, "Abba, Father".'

Abba

Perhaps the most remarkable thing about these verses is Paul's use of the word 'Abba', when he is referring to the Christian calling out to God. It is remarkable because it is an Aramaic word. Galatians is a letter written in Greek to people who speak Greek, but not (mostly at least) Aramaic. Why then does Paul tell them that the Holy Spirit inspires Christians to call out 'Abba', going on to translate it for them as 'Father'? The answer is simple: the word came from Jesus, whose first language was Aramaic. Mark's gospel confirms that Jesus used the term: Mark describes Jesus in the garden of Gethsemane struggling with the fearful prospect of crucifixion, and saying 'Abba, Father ... take this cup from me' (Mark

63

14.36). Mark, like Paul, is writing in Greek, but specifically records the Aramaic word.

This suggests that it was an unusual way of addressing God. If it was the normal way of addressing God that lots of people used, then we would not expect the Greek-speaking writers of the New Testament specifically to recall the Aramaic term as something Jesus used. In fact the evidence is that the Jews of Jesus' day did not normally speak of God as Abba. 'Abba' was the way that children in families would address their father. It was not quite as childish a word as the English 'Daddy', but still it probably sounded over-familiar to the Jews, who were very sensitive about taking God or his name lightly. Jesus, however, used it; it expressed something of his closeness to God, and people remembered it as something striking and distinctive about Jesus.

But how do we know that Paul took the expression from Jesus? First, because he uses the Aramaic in a Greek letter, and second because he specifically refers to God sending 'the Spirit *of his Son* into our hearts, the Spirit who calls out, *Abba*' (4.6; see also Romans 8.15–16).

Here then is strong evidence that Paul knew about the ministry of Jesus and about Jesus having a striking sense of being God's Son; furthermore, when he uses the term 'Abba', Paul takes it for granted that the Galatians will understand what he is talking about. It is by no means impossible that they knew the Gethsemane story in particular, since it is here that Mark has Jesus use the expression. We shall see when we come to 1 Corinthians that Paul refers there to 'The Lord Jesus on the night he was betrayed' (11.23), which was the night of Gethsemane according to the gospels (see e.g. Mark 14.36).

Born of a woman

But the verses we have just quoted from Galatians speak of God sending his Son in the fulness of time, 'born of a woman, born under law'. Does this suggest that Paul knew the stories of Jesus' birth? Three things are interesting about what Paul says here.

First, he refers to Jesus being born of a woman. Is there any significance in the fact that he refers to Jesus' mother, but not his father? If Paul knew the stories of Jesus' birth in something like the form we find them in Matthew and Luke, with Mary conceiving 'by the Holy Spirit', then it could well be that he chose his words carefully here. On the other hand, it was an expression that could be used of other human figures: Jesus, for example, can speak of John the Baptist as greater than anyone else born of woman (Matthew 11.11).

Second, the Greek word rendered 'born' in the translation we have followed is not the regular word for being born. Paul uses the regular word later in the very same chapter when he talks about Isaac and Ishmael and their mothers (4.21–31); that is a word that suggests being born of a human father and mother (*gennaoomai*; compare Matthew 1.1–16, where the verb is used in the genealogy of fathers 'begetting' children). But in 4.4, when speaking of Jesus, Paul uses a somewhat similar-sounding, but more general word that means something like 'become' (*ginomai*). We could translate this verb 'coming forth of a woman', and see no particular significance in Paul's choice of term. On the other hand, it may be significant that Paul never uses the regular word of Jesus' birth, but here and also in Romans 1.3 and Philippians 2.7 he uses the 'become' word. Was this because he knew that Jesus was not fathered by Joseph?

Third, the whole phraseology of Galatians 4.4, 'When the time had fully come, God sent his Son, born of a woman, born under law, to redeem those under law', is strongly reminiscent of Luke's account of Jesus' birth in his chapters 1 and 2. Those chapters

- have a strong sense of the time of God's salvation having come;
- speak of Jesus as God's Son (1.32, 35);
- focus on Mary his mother;
- emphasize that Mary and Joseph faithfully observed the Jewish laws about childbirth (2.21–7);
- speak of Jesus as the one who has come to redeem Israel (1.68, 2.38).

Those three points together might well suggest to the detective that Paul knows the story. This would not be surprising, if the author of Luke was a companion of Paul, which is what is suggested by the author's second volume, Acts (notice the 'we' in chapters 16–28). Of course, the relationship could be the opposite way round, with the author of Luke–Acts developing Paul's brief statements into a colourful narrative. But that is not the way round with

'Abba', and it is not the obvious way round with Paul's other references to Jesus in these verses: for example, it was not particularly convenient for Paul that Jesus was 'born under law, to redeem those under law', since he was arguing against people who were trying to impose the law on Gentiles. But the point would have been unavoidable if he and others knew infancy stories such as are found in Luke's gospel.

The Spirit of the Son in our hearts

Paul emphasizes that Christians are 'sons' of God, and so 'God sent the Spirit of his Son into our hearts, the Spirit who calls out *Abba*' (4.6). We have explored the importance of the term *Abba*, as something that was distinctive of Jesus. But Paul speaks in this verse of the Galatians sharing in Jesus' sonship and so in the Spirit of his Son. When Paul speaks of sonship, he is not being sexist or excluding women; on the contrary, just a few verses before he makes the point that there is no male and female in Christ (3.28); he speaks of sonship to make the point that we all have been united to Jesus the Son.

In those previous verses he makes it clear that this experience of sonship comes through faith in Christ Jesus, a faith expressed through baptism (3.26–7). Paul speaks of 'baptism into Christ' and of the baptized person having 'clothed themselves with Christ'. For Paul, in baptism we become one with Christ and in Christ; we belong to him and with him. As we saw before, Paul sees us as sharing in Jesus' death – 'being crucified with Christ': we haven't literally been crucified, but we have been united to Jesus, who was, and so his crucifixion is now ours (by faith), as is his Spirit.

The link between baptism, sonship and the Spirit also reminds us of the gospel story of Jesus' own baptism by John the Baptist in the river Jordan. When Jesus was baptized, the gospels record that the Holy Spirit was seen descending on him like a dove, and a voice from heaven said 'You are my Son' (Mark 1.9–11). A real possibility must be that Paul's understanding of Christian baptism derives from that story of Jesus' baptism – ultimately, at any rate.

Scholars have pointed out that it is unlikely that Christians invented the story of Jesus being baptized by John the Baptist, since it was arguably a somewhat embarrassing story for Christians:

it was potentially embarrassing that their master was baptized by someone else, almost as if he were that person's disciple, and it was potentially embarrassing to have their master undergoing a baptism for the forgiveness of sins – as if he needed it (cf. Matthew 3.14–15; John 1.20, 3.27–30). So Jesus was surely baptized by John, and this must have been the route by which baptism came into the Christian church.

What seems likely then is that the story of Jesus' baptism became the model for Christian baptism, except that Jesus is the original and believers come to share in his life and experience – of the Spirit and of Sonship, as well as of death and resurrection. There is no proof that Paul knew the baptism stories, but it is a plausible inference (2 Corinthians 1.21–2 is further evidence pointing in that direction).

The kingdom of God

What else did Paul know of Jesus and teach to the Galatians? The gospels are clear that Jesus' teaching centred on the coming of the kingdom of God. Jesus announced that 'the time is fulfilled, the kingdom of God has come near' (so Mark 1.15). Scholars have argued vigorously about his exact meaning. What seems most likely is that Jesus was announcing the time promised in the Old Testament when God would intervene to save his people, when evil would be overthrown, and when God's reign over the world (the kingdom of God in that sense) would be re-established in the world.

Paul reflects this sort of thinking at various points in Galatians, as, for example, when he says that Jesus came 'when the time had been fulfilled' (4.4), and when he speaks of Jesus as the one who came to 'rescue us from the present evil age' (1.4). But Paul does not often refer to the kingdom of God in his letters. This may partly be because it was a rather Jewish concept, which would not have rung such clear bells with his Greek-speaking hearers and readers.

However, in Galatians 5.21, having spoken of various human sins – from sexual immorality to 'drunkenness, orgies, and the like', he says: 'I warn you, as I warned you before, that those who live like this will not inherit the kingdom of God.' Three things are interesting about this:

1. Paul drops in this reference to 'inheriting the kingdom of God' without explanation, assuming that his readers will understand what he means.
2. He specifically says that he has warned them in these terms before (which confirms the previous point).
3. Questions about entering or inheriting the kingdom of God are very important in the teaching of Jesus in the gospels: the Sermon on the Mount, for example, speaks of the kingdom of heaven (or God) belonging to the poor in spirit, and also to those persecuted for righteousness' sake; it speaks of the meek 'inheriting' the earth (Matthew 5.3–10). The kingdom of God is also explicitly associated with righteousness, for example in Matthew 5.20: 'Unless your righteousness surpasses that of the Pharisees and teachers of the law, you will certainly not enter the kingdom of heaven.' In Matthew 25 the 'sheep' in Jesus' parable of the sheep and the goats are identified as 'the righteous' (v. 37) and are invited to 'inherit the kingdom prepared for you' (v. 34). Paul assumes a similar connection between the kingdom and righteousness in 1 Corinthians 6.9–10, where he asks: 'Do you not know that the unrighteous will not inherit the kingdom of God?'; he goes on to contrast the unrighteous with the Corinthian Christians, who have been washed, sanctified and 'made righteous' in the name of the Lord Jesus. His question 'Do you not know?' implies that they should know, because, I suggest, they had been specifically taught about the kingdom of God.

We will return to the question of the kingdom of God in our consideration of 1 Corinthians. But we can conclude even at this stage that Paul did know Jesus' teaching about the kingdom of God, and that he had passed it on to the Galatians (as he would to the Corinthians).

The apostles

Jesus shared his ministry with the twelve apostles, according to the gospels, and it is very clear from Galatians that apostleship was something very important to Paul. He regarded the apostles as a special group (1.19), and he saw himself as an apostle (see 1.1: 'Paul, an apostle – sent not from men nor by man, but by Jesus Christ and God the Father'; also 1.17, 2.8).

Galatians 1 and 2 make it clear that not everyone saw Paul in that way; his critics saw him as a second-hand Christian leader, inferior to and dependent on the real apostles. The real apostles were those who were with Jesus and sent out by him. (The word 'apostle' means literally 'sent one'.) Paul vigorously rejects their demotion of him, arguing both that he had a personal revelation of Jesus and that he was commissioned to go to the Gentiles (1.13–17; cf. 1.1). He takes up the theme explicitly in 1 Corinthians. He asks: 'Am I not an apostle? Have I not seen Jesus our Lord?' (9.1) and he refers to the risen Jesus appearing to various people and 'last of all he appeared to me, as to one abnormally born. For I am the least of the apostles' (15.7–9).

Paul knows not just about the apostles in general, but about Peter in particular, as someone who had a special position of leadership among the apostles. He also knows that they, and Peter in particular, had a specific mission to go to the Jews, as opposed to the Gentiles (Galatians 2.6–9). It is interesting to see how Paul seems to compare himself with Peter (2.7, 8).

From all of this it seems probable that Paul knew of Jesus' special commissioning of Peter. One real possibility is that he knew the story recorded in Matthew 16.16–20, where Peter declares Jesus to be the Christ, the Son of the living God, and where Jesus congratulates him with the words 'Blessed are you, Simon son of Jonah, for this was not revealed to you by flesh and blood, but by my Father in heaven. And I tell you that you are Peter, and on this rock I will build my church'. What is interesting is that the phraseology used here about the 'revealing' of 'the Son' by God, not by 'flesh and blood', is very similar to that used by Paul of his own conversion in Galatians 1.13–17. It is at least possible that Paul is telling the story of his conversion in a way that brings out the parallel between himself and Peter; certainly he compares himself to Peter in what follows. He may well be doing something similar in 1 Corinthians 15.3–8, where he refers to Peter as the first to see the risen Jesus and to himself as the last. It is interesting if Paul does know the sayings of Matthew 16.16–20, because they only occur in

Matthew's gospel and not in Mark, which is usually believed to be the first gospel to have been written. Some scholars conclude that they are not original sayings of Jesus; Paul, however, may be an early witness to Matthew's account.

Paul may also support Matthew's account of Jesus in his reference to Peter and the others being sent 'to the circumcised', since in Matthew's gospel alone Jesus tells the disciples not to go to the Gentiles and the Samaritans, but only 'to the lost sheep of Israel' (10.6). Matthew also has Jesus speak of his own mission in similarly restrictive terms (15.24). Since these references are not in Mark and Luke, some scholars think they don't go back to Jesus. But it is easy to see why Mark and Luke might have left those sayings of Jesus out, since they were both writing for Gentiles, who could have been perplexed by Jesus' apparent lack of interest in them. Paul seems to support Matthew both in Galatians 2, where he speaks of Peter and the others being apostles to the Jews (v. 9), and in Romans 15, where he speaks of Jesus as a 'servant to the circumcised' (v. 8), and more generally in Romans, where he speaks of the Christian good news being 'for the Jew first and also for the Greek' (e.g. 1.16). It would not have been in Paul's interests to invent the idea of Jesus and the apostles giving priority to the Jews; it must be that he knows this to have been the case.

We may conclude that Paul knew various of the gospel sayings about the apostles, a point to which we will return in our discussion of 1 Corinthians in Chapter 14.

One final point on Galatians and the apostles: Paul seems to know that Peter had a pre-eminent position among the apostles, but he also speaks of James, Peter and John as the 'pillars' of the church in Jerusalem, or at least as those who 'seemed' or 'were reputed to be' pillars (2.9). We may guess that Paul's opponents were putting Paul down and emphasizing the 'pillars' – to Paul's irritation.

But why were they called the 'pillars'? A likely enough guess is that behind the expression lies the picture of the Church as a temple, the three apostles concerned being seen as 'pillars' in it (cf. 1 Corinthians 3.16; 2 Corinthians 5.16; Revelation 3.12). But why were these three in particular seen as 'pillars'? An intriguing possible answer is suggested by the gospels, because they portray Jesus as having had an inner group of three apostles to whom he was particularly close, namely Peter, James and John. Is it possible that, just as Peter was nicknamed the 'rock' by Jesus according to Matthew 16.18, so he and his companions came to be nicknamed the 'pillars' – because of their special closeness to Jesus and their involvement in some of the momentous events of his life (including the Transfiguration and the spiritual struggle in the Garden of Gethsemane, e.g. Mark 9.2, 14.33)?

This suggestion may be supported by the rather mysterious saying of Jesus just before the Transfiguration, when he speaks of 'some standing here who will not taste death before they see the kingdom of God having come with power' (Mark 9.1). Two things are significant about this saying: first, in Aramaic the word for 'pillar' means literally something like 'standing one'; second, it seems likely that Mark, Matthew and Luke saw the Transfiguration as the fulfilment of Jesus' promise that some of the 'standing ones' (the pillars?) would see the kingdom of God, which Jesus had come to bring, in amazing power. (This is suggested among other things by the way in which the gospels connect the saying chronologically with the Transfiguration – after six or eight days).

So does Paul's reference to the 'pillars' lead us back ultimately to the Transfiguration story? There are some possible echoes of the story elsewhere in Paul's writings, notably in 2 Corinthians 3 and 4, where Paul speaks about the glory experienced by Moses on Mount Sinai being superseded by Christ. He speaks of Christians being 'transfigured' by our relationship with Christ (3.18), and of God's light shining in our hearts and giving us 'the light of the knowledge of the glory of God in the face of Christ' (4.6). Paul may well here be referring to his conversion experience, but perhaps also alluding to the Transfiguration event. Did Paul perhaps see his conversion as his equivalent of the disciples' mountain-top experience?

These suggestions about the 'pillars' and the Transfiguration may seem too ingenious by far. And there is a problem: namely that the James of Jesus' ministry had been executed by Herod Agrippa *before* Paul came to Jerusalem and met up with the 'pillars' (Acts 12.2). The pillar James whom he met was Jesus' brother, who seems to have taken over the leadership of the Jerusalem church at the time of Herod's violent persecution of the Christians. So is the idea about the 'pillars' as Jesus' inner three disciples a false lead?

Perhaps. But it is possible that when James the apostle was executed, James the brother came effectively to take his place in the leading triumvirate of the Church, in which case the argument would still hold; or that James the brother had in any case been included in the inner circle even before the death of the apostle.

Mention of the disciples James and John may remind us of the occasion when the two apostles are said to have approached Jesus and asked for top seats in his kingdom (Mark 10.35–45). Jesus in his reply talks about those who 'seem to be' or 'are reputed to be' leaders of the Gentiles lording it over them; 'Not so with you' (10.43). The Greek word used here for 'seem'/'are reputed to be' is the same used by Paul when he speaks of those who 'seem to be' or 'who have the reputation of being' pillars (Galatians 2.6, 9). Is it possible that Paul, in reacting negatively to his opponents who are putting him down and setting up Peter, James and John as the real apostles, is calling to mind the story of Jesus, who rejected the human way of setting people up on pedestals? This is at best a faint clue, though we shall see further evidence of Paul's knowledge of the story of Jesus, James and John in due course (in Chapter 14).

The destruction of the temple and being crucified with Christ

We speculated that the 'pillars' imagery could have something to do with the temple, because is clear from Paul's later letters that he sees the Christian church as the temple of the Holy Spirit (1 Corinthians 3.16; 2 Corinthians 6.16). This understanding of the Church is remarkable, given the significance of the temple in Jewish thinking and given that the temple was still standing and functioning in Jerusalem (though there is a partial parallel in the Dead Sea Scrolls). How did Paul and others come to this view?

It is likely that two things will have contributed. First, Jesus and the temple came into conflict. Many scholars think that it was Jesus' actions and words against the temple that above all infuriated the Jewish leaders in Jerusalem, and led to his death. His entry into the temple and throwing over of the tables was certainly provocative, and was a prophetic type of action that spoke of the judgement of God on this corrupt institution (Mark 11.12–33). The gospels suggest that it was Jesus' prediction of the destruction of the temple that was particularly held against him in his trial, even if the powers that be misunderstood his meaning (Mark 14.58, etc.).

But, if the first thing that led to the Christian rejection of the temple was Jesus' criticism of it, the other thing seems to have been the death of Jesus. The Christians' explanation of the death of their Messiah was that it was a divinely ordained sacrifice for sin, and if it was such, then the major *raison d'être* of the temple as a place of sacrifice was arguably at an end; Jesus' body on the cross had displaced the temple. This is presumably part of the significance of the tearing of the temple curtain, which Matthew, Mark and Luke describe as occurring immediately after the death of Jesus (Mark 15.38, etc.); the temple is no longer the God-given way to forgiveness and to God.

But what has this to do with Galatians? The answer is that it may lie behind Galatians 2.17–21, where Paul warns Peter that by withdrawing from fellowship with Gentiles he is in danger of 'rebuilding' what has been 'destroyed'. The 'destroying'/'rebuilding' language is exactly what is used in Jesus' saying as quoted at his trial, where Jesus is accused of promising to 'destroy this temple' and 'in three days build it again' (Matthew 26.61; Mark 14.58). It has been plausibly argued that Paul is saying to Peter that by reinstating the law, which is what Paul sees him as doing by agreeing to the demands of the 'circumcision' party, he is undoing the work of Jesus on the cross. Jesus died to bring freedom from the law and the temple regime, but Peter is in danger of reinstating them, and making Jesus' death pointless (Galatians 2.21). That is unthinkable for Paul, 'for I have been crucified with Christ' (2.20).

As for crucifixion with Christ, we have seen how Paul saw this as involved in Christian baptism, sharing in the death of Jesus. Whether he derived the idea simply by associating the dramatic rite of baptism (going under and coming up) with the death and resurrection of Jesus, or by reflection on the crucifixion itself, when sinners were crucified with Jesus, is impossible to say. Another possibility is that he was influenced by Jesus' challenge to his disciples about the need to deny themselves and 'to take up the cross' and follow him. This saying of Jesus is attested several times in the gospels (e.g. in Mark 8.34). It is a shocking statement, given the contemporary practice of crucifixion. But it may well have been important to Paul's view of baptism: if Jesus said that discipleship involved saying goodbye to oneself and taking up the cross with Jesus, then it makes sense that baptism, as the moment of commitment to Jesus, is described by Paul as being 'into the death of Jesus' (Romans 6.3); it makes sense that Paul can speak of being 'crucified with Christ' and say that 'it is no longer I who live' (Galatians 2.20).

We conclude that Galatians 2.17–21, where Paul speaks of rebuilding and destroying and of being crucified with Christ, may well reflect Paul's knowledge of Jesus' difficult sayings about the temple and about taking up the cross. The evidence is not conclusive, but certainly suggestive.

Love and the law

Paul's emphasis on love as the first fruit of the Spirit, and his comment on love as summing up the whole law (Galatians 5.14, 22), has much in common with Jesus' teaching on love. According to the gospels Jesus summed up the law in terms of love and emphasized love of neighbour and love of one's enemies (e.g. Mark 12.29–31; Matthew 5.43).

The verse in Galatians that explicitly points back to Jesus is 6.2, where Paul urges the Galatians to 'bear each other's burdens, and so you will fulfil the law of Christ'. What does Paul have in mind when he speaks of 'the law of Christ'? Does he just have in mind that love was the way of Jesus, seen above all in the cross (2.20), and that this is therefore the Christian way? He might mean that, but why then does he use the word 'law'?

It seems more likely that he has in mind the teaching of Jesus, and it could very well be that he is referring back to the story in the gospels where Jesus specifically highlights the Old Testament command to 'love your neighbour as yourself' (Mark 12.31; Matthew 22.39). This is all the more likely, given that this Old Testament verse is quoted by Paul just a few verses before in 5.14, and given that Paul describes the 'love' command as fulfilling the whole law, as in Matthew's version of the words of Jesus he says, 'All the law and the prophets hang on these two commandments' (the first being the command to love God).

However, although it does seem likely that Paul knows these words of Jesus and echoes them in Galatians 5.14, it is not an entirely adequate explanation of Galatians 6.2, where Paul speaks of carrying each others' burdens as fulfilling 'the law of Christ'. It is not adequate, first, because the words of Jesus about loving one's neighbour are not exactly about bearing one another's burdens, and, second, because it does not really make sense for Paul to call a perfectly good Old Testament law, which Jesus simply endorsed, 'the law of Christ'. It would be different if it were something more distinctive of Jesus.

The more likely explanation emerges from a closer look at Galatians 5.14, because Paul's quotation of the 'love your neighbour' text follows and backs up Paul's preceding command to the Galatians: 'through love be slaves of one another' (5.13). And here we have something important and distinctive of Jesus, namely his emphasis on service within the Christian fellowship. In the passage we have already mentioned about James and John asking for the top seats in the kingdom, Jesus tells his disciples that that is not to be their way; they are to take the lowest place, ' whoever wants to be great among you must be your servant, and whoever wants to be first must be slave of all' (Mark 10.43–4). It is surely this teaching of Jesus that Paul has in mind as the 'law of Christ'; we shall see further evidence of the importance of this teaching when we look at 1 Corinthians.

But there is one more piece to fit into this jigsaw. Why does Paul call this 'the *law* of Christ', in a letter where he has been emphasizing Christian freedom from the law? Why does he not speak of 'the way' or 'the teaching' of Christ? A possible answer is suggested by John's gospel, where Jesus says to his disciples that he is giving them 'a new commandment', and this 'new commandment' is 'love one another, as I have loved you' (John 13.34). What such love means in the context of John's gospel is suggested when Jesus washes the disciples' feet, and then supremely exhibited when he goes to the cross (John 13.1–17, 15.12–13); the disciples' love for one another is to be expressed in humble self-sacrificial service, as exemplified by Jesus. The parallel between this teaching in John and Mark 10 is unmistakable, since there too the model of service for the disciples is the Son of Man giving his life for others (10.45). The command to love in John's gospel and the call to serve in the synoptic gospels turn out to be very closely related indeed.

But how does the evidence from John cast light on Paul's reference to 'the law of Christ'? The answer is simple: Paul, we suggested, had Jesus' call to self-sacrificial service in mind when he spoke of the law of Christ; John says that Jesus himself spoke explicitly of such self-sacrificial love as '*his*' distinctive and new '*commandment*'. The logical conclusion is that Paul had Jesus' words about the new commandment in mind when he spoke of 'bearing one another's burdens' as a way of fulfilling 'the law of Christ'. It could theoretically be a coincidence that John and Paul encourage Christians to care 'for one another' and that both identify this as a distinctive 'law'/'commandment' of Christ; but it is more likely that Paul's unusual usage reflects his knowledge of the words of Jesus which John records.

This conclusion is fascinating, since John's gospel is usually seen as the last to have been written and is often regarded as a theologically coloured account rather than good history. But Paul at this point seems to attest to the Johannine account of Jesus. Some scholars have suspected this also in the famous hymn of Philippians 2, where Paul's description of Christ taking the form of a servant and humbling himself, even to death, is reminiscent of John 13, where Jesus performs the servant's role in washing the disciples' feet, just before going on to his death.

Our detective work in Galatians has taken us in all sorts of interesting directions. Some of the clues and arguments are very uncertain, for example the argument about those 'reputed to be pillars'; but other clues and arguments are much less ambiguous, for example the arguments about the cross, about Abba, and even about 'the law of Christ'. The overall conclusion is that there is a lot of evidence suggesting that Paul knew and taught the Galatians about Jesus' life, ministry, death and resurrection. This would fit in with the small amount of evidence from Acts, which suggests that Paul did teach about the life of Jesus from John the Baptist through to his death and resurrection. But what we have looked at in this chapter is only the evidence from one of Paul's letters, and we have a lot more ground to cover before the case is complete.

8 Travelling in Greece

On the way there

Having taken a breather from Paul's travels and reflected on Galatians, we need now to take up the story again. Paul was very upset at the time of writing Galatians, upset by what was happening to 'his' churches in Galatia, and upset by what he saw as betrayal by Peter and even Barnabas. But then the Jerusalem Council was convened, as Acts 15 records, and its decisions brilliantly accommodated the differing concerns of Paul and Peter and Barnabas.

Acts says that Paul and Barnabas then returned to Antioch, with two additional delegates from the Jerusalem church, Judas and Silas, 'who said much to encourage and strengthen the brothers' (15.32). It is not difficult to imagine that such encouragement might have been needed after what had happened, and it may be significant that Acts then tells us that they were sent back to Jerusalem 'with peace' (15.33). They had helped to bring peace, and were sent off in peace.

But things did not remain entirely harmonious: Acts describes another argument between Paul and Barnabas, which arose when Paul wanted to take to the road again and to revisit the churches of Galatia. This time the argument was over John Mark: Barnabas wished to take him with them, but Paul, recalling how Mark had given up last time in Pamphylia, was unwilling to take someone he saw as unreliable. The result was a 'sharp disagreement' and a parting of the ways, Barnabas taking Mark to revisit Cyprus and Paul taking Silas and going overland this time to Syria, Cilicia (the Tarsus area) and Galatia (15.36–41).

This all makes good historical sense. The author of Acts, for whom both Barnabas and Paul were heroes, would hardly have invented this clash. And, although Paul's letters do not speak of the clash, Galatians shows that there had been tensions between Paul and Barnabas, and Paul's letters to the Thessalonians confirm that the next stage of his ministry was in collaboration with Silas (or

Silvanus) (1 Thessalonians 1.1; 2 Thessalonians 1.1). It makes good sense that Barnabas should have headed back to his home, Cyprus, and that Paul should have gone in the direction of his home Tarsus.

When Paul came to Galatia, he visited Derbe and Lystra, where he recruited Timothy to his missionary team (16.1–5). Interestingly, Acts says that Paul 'circumcised him because of the Jews who lived in that area'. This may seem unlikely: that in Galatia of all places the author of Galatians should circumcise an uncircumcised Christian 'because of the Jews'! The author of Acts is aware that it may seem surprising, but explains that 'his mother was a Jewess and a believer, but his father was a Greek', and implies that Timothy's uncircumcision was a barrier or offence to the Jews of the area. Paul therefore sees it as desirable for his ministry to have him circumcised, not because circumcision was important for salvation, but because it would be helpful for mission and ministry.

It is true that it is hard to imagine Paul doing this when writing Galatians, but since then the matter had been discussed in detail at the Council of Jerusalem: Paul's point of principle about Gentiles being free from the law had been accepted at the Council, but so had the concerns of others about good relations with the Jews (15.21). Paul had no problem with the latter concern, and indeed in his later letters he advocates accommodation to the tender consciences of Jews (1 Corinthians 9.20; Romans 14). So the Acts account of Paul circumcising Timothy makes perfectly good sense: Paul was much more relaxed about the whole issue than he had been (even in Galatians he had said that 'neither circumcision nor uncircumcision counts for anything': 6.15); and he probably felt that Timothy's ambiguous status as a half-Jew made his circumcision desirable as a special case. The deliberate mention of it in Acts confirms that it was a special case.

After ministry in Galatia, Paul and his growing team moved on. Acts says that they tried to enter Asia (west of Galatia, with its capital Ephesus) and also Bithynia (in the north of Turkey on the Black Sea coast), but 'the Spirit of Jesus would not allow them to' (16.6–7). Quite what form this prohibition took we are not told, but prophets play a large part in the Acts account, and it may well have been a prophetic word that helped guide their decisions. Eventually they came to Troas on the north-west coast of Turkey, where according to Acts Paul had a vision of a 'man from Macedonia' inviting him to come to Macedonia in north Greece, which is what they did (16.9).

Acts suggests that Paul's ministry had a major 'prophetic' or more broadly 'charismatic' dimension to it. Prophets seem to be frequently involved, and Acts describes Paul as having both visions and spiritual power, manifested in healings and other powerful signs (13.11, 14.3, 10). Galatians confirms this picture: Paul speaks there not only of having his own life-changing revelation of Jesus, but also of going up to Jerusalem by revelation (2.2); he also refers to the Galatians' own powerful experiences of the Spirit (3.5). These aspects of early church life will become even more prominent in his later letters. One particularly interesting passage is in 2 Corinthians 12, where Paul speaks of his 'visions and revelations from the Lord', and then goes on to describe 'a man in Christ who fourteen years ago was caught up to the third heaven. Whether it was in the body or out of the body I do not know' (12.1–2). He is evidently referring here to himself, though he is embarrassed at 'boasting' of his spiritual experiences. The 'fourteen years ago' would take us back to quite an early stage in Paul's ministry, perhaps to his time in Tarsus before he was recruited to work in Antioch by Barnabas. Paul had a particularly remarkable mystical experience at that time, but it sounds as though visions and revelations were a regular characteristic of his ministry (12.7).

Ministry in Greece according to Acts

Philippi

The crossing of the sea from Troas to Macedonia (and Europe, as we see it today) was no doubt a momentous step for Paul. It represented a move into the Greek heartlands. Acts describes Paul ministering in Philippi, 'the first city of the district' (16.12). It was not in fact the capital of the area, but it was a Roman colony, situated on the great trunk road, the Via Egnatia, and was in many ways more important than the capital Amphipolis. In Philippi there appears to have been no synagogue, presumably because there were not many Jews there; but Acts describes Paul and Silas meeting up with the Jews at their worship place by the river outside the city. Paul and Silas on this occasion did not fall foul of the Jews, but they ran into trouble when Paul exorcised a spirit-possessed slave girl, who had been making money for her owners by fortune-telling. Paul and Silas were on this occasion accused of being Jews, who 'are throwing our city into an uproar by advocating customs unlawful for us Romans to accept or practise' (16.20). The upshot was that they were flogged and put in prison by the authorities; but they were later released through a massive earthquake (the area is earthquake-prone); this led to the conversion of their jailer, and the authorities backed down when they heard that Paul and Silas were Roman citizens.

Thessalonica

Paul and Silas went on from Philippi to the important coastal city of Thessalonica, where there was a Jewish synagogue (17.1). Acts describes them speaking in the synagogue on three sabbaths, arguing for Jesus being the Christ (17.3). The response was, as so often in Galatia, mixed: some of the Jews and 'a large number of God-fearing Greeks and not a few prominent women' joined Paul and Silas, but others were 'jealous' and incited a riot against Paul. Such 'jealousy' is easy to understand: for the synagogue leaders to see their members and their influential supporters being siphoned off into the new Christian movement must have been disturbing, to say the least. Paul's host, Jason, and some others were arrested, and brought before the authorities (the 'politarchs', as Acts correctly describes them); the Christians were accused of international trouble-making and of proclaiming a rival emperor to Caesar, i.e. Jesus. Paul and Silas seem to have avoided arrest but, presumably for their own safety, were 'sent away' by night by the Christians in Thessalonica, and moved on to the next city of Berea (17.1–9).

Berea

In Berea Paul and Silas went to the synagogue, and Acts suggests that they had a much more sympathetic reception than in Thessalonica. However, eventually Jews from Thessalonica made their way to Berea, and started making life difficult for Paul once again. So once again Paul was on his way, escorted by some of the Berean

Christians to Athens; Silas and Timothy stayed in Berea, though Paul instructed them to join him as soon as possible (17.10–15).

Athens

It is not hard to imagine what an awesome experience it must have been for Paul to arrive in the historic and beautiful city of Athens, perhaps a rather frightening experience, especially with his companions left behind in Berea. Acts describes Paul reasoning in the synagogue and in the market place day by day, but gives the impression that the response was modest: Luke mentions two people, Dionysius and Damaris, 'and a number of others' who responded positively (17.34).

Most interesting is Acts' description of Paul's discussions with some Athenian philosophers. They were intrigued about the 'foreign gods' he was advocating: Acts explains that Paul was preaching 'Jesus and the resurrection'. It is just possible that they thought that Jesus was the name of one deity and 'resurrection', *anastasis* in Greek, the name of another. In any case they brought Paul to the ancient Areopagus Court to explain his ideas to the leading citizens of Athens who comprised the court. Paul's speech is only the second 'evangelistic' address by Paul recorded in Acts, and it is (not surprisingly) totally different from the address to the synagogue in Iconium (in chapter 13). Paul talks to the Greeks about their altars and idols, commenting on an altar 'to an unknown God', and speaking to them of the living God, who made the world and in whom 'we live and move and have our being'. The last phrase appears to be a quotation from the sixth century BC Cretan poet Epimenides. Paul proceeds to tell the Athenians to repent, because God is going to judge the world through 'a man he has appointed'; Paul means Jesus, of course, and he refers to the resurrection as his evidence (17.16–31).

Corinth

Paul then left Athens and went further south to Corinth, another famous city standing on an isthmus four or five miles wide between the Aegean Sea and the Adriatic. Corinth was a Roman colony, and a major centre for trade. There is now a canal across the isthmus; then there was only a slipway across which small ships could be towed, or goods could be unloaded and transported by land from Cenchreae, the city's eastern port, to Lechaeum, its western port. Corinth was famous for sport – the Isthmian Games – and for religion, the city being dominated by the huge temple of Aphrodite (the goddess of love) on the immediately adjacent mountain-top, and full of other temples.

Acts tells us that Paul stayed there with a Jewish couple, Aquila and Priscilla, and worked with them at his tent-making trade. Acts tells us that they had come recently from Italy, 'because Claudius had ordered all the Jews to leave Rome' (18.1–3). This expulsion of Jews by the Roman emperor is also mentioned by the Roman historian Suetonius, who explains that it was because 'the Jews were rioting at the instigation of Chrestus' (*Life of Claudius* 25.4). Suetonius does not say more, but a probable explanation is that 'Chrestus' means Christ, and it seems likely that the expulsion was in response to major disturbances within the Jewish community caused by the growing Christian missionary movement. We have seen how much trouble the Christian movement caused in Galatia and elsewhere, and it looks as though this was replicated in Rome, where there was a large Jewish population, estimated by some as between 40 and 50 thousand out of a total of one million. The authorities in Rome will presumably have been aware of the trouble the Christian movement had been causing in other Jewish communities in various parts of the empire (cf. Acts 17.6); when these troubles reached the capital itself, the emperor acted decisively and expelled the Jews from the city. It seems quite likely that Aquila and Priscilla were Jewish Christians, perhaps leaders in the burgeoning Roman church, who had been caught up in the expulsion. In any case, Acts describes Paul as joining them in Corinth.

Paul's strategy in Corinth was the same as elsewhere; he began his evangelism in the synagogue. The response was also similar, some Jews being converted, including a leading member of the synagogue, Crispus, others growing hostile, forcing Paul to move his centre of operations to 'the house of Titius Justus', a sympathetic God-fearing Gentile. Acts describes one particular time when the Jewish hostility against Paul grew so intense that he was brought to the proconsul (i.e. governor) of the region, Gallio. Gallio was uninterested in what he saw as an intra-Jewish wrangle, and we are told that he dismissed the case, leaving Sosthenes, the leader of the synagogue, to be beaten up by a hostile crowd (who presumably resented the Jewish 'trouble-making' in the city). Despite his lack of interest in Paul, from our point of view Gallio is interesting, because archaeological evidence shows that he was proconsul of Achaia in the years AD 50–2. The expulsion of the Jews from Rome probably occurred in AD 49. So we have a very important chronological clue here. Acts suggests that Paul stayed in Corinth for at least a year and a half (18.11) and quite probably longer (18.18). While he was there he was rejoined by Silas and Timothy.

Ministry in Greece according to Paul's letters

Such is the story of Paul in Greece, as told by Acts. To what extent do Paul's letters confirm the story? The very fact that the New Testament contains letters addressed by Paul to the churches in Philippi, Thessalonica and Corinth confirms that Paul had a significant ministry in each of those places. It is interesting that both letters to Thessalonica come from 'Paul, Silas and Timothy' (1 Thessalonians 1.1; 2 Thessalonians 1.1), Philippians and 2 Corinthians come from 'Paul and Timothy' (Philippians 1.1; 2 Corinthians 1.1) and 1 Corinthians from 'Paul and Sosthenes' (1 Corinthians 1.1). This all fits in with the evidence of Acts about Paul's co-workers in those places. The exception is Sosthenes; but it is an intriguing possibility that he is the second synagogue ruler mentioned in Acts' description of Paul's ministry in Corinth (17.16; cp. v. 8), in which case two leaders of the synagogue in Corinth were converted to Christianity, and Sosthenes subsequently joined Paul on his missionary travels.

1 Thessalonians written from Corinth

The most interesting evidence bearing on the Acts story is in 1 Thessalonians, because it was evidently written quite soon after Paul's visit to the Thessalonians, probably when Paul was in Corinth. The evidence for this includes the following:

- his comments on his visit to them and on their conversion in chapter 1, as though it was something quite recent;

83

- his description in 2.17 about how he had been separated from them for a short time and his comments about how anxious he was for their spiritual welfare;
- his reference in chapter 3 to being in Athens alone and to sending Timothy to them;
- his joy and thankfulness for Timothy's good news and return.

1 Thessalonians, however, does raise a few questions when compared with Acts. 1 Thessalonians refers to Paul sending Timothy to Thessalonica from Athens after he got there (3.2); but Acts suggests that Silas and Timothy stayed in the Thessalonica area when Paul went on to Athens and that they both joined Paul in Corinth after his time in Athens (17.14, 18.5). However, this is a small discrepancy in two accounts that fit generally very well. It may be that Silas and Timothy stayed in Berea at first, as Acts suggests, but then Timothy visited Paul in Athens, without this being noted in Acts. Or it may be that only Silas stayed in Berea and that Timothy accompanied Paul to Athens; Timothy went back, however, at Paul's bidding, and rejoined Silas. In this case the writer of Acts may have oversimplified slightly, not mentioning all the toing and froing that went on; but he is quite right to have Silas and Timothy staying on in the Thessalonica area after Paul had left, and then to have them both join Paul in Corinth (1 Thessalonians is written when both of them are present with Paul).

We may rather confidently conclude that 1 Thessalonians was written from Corinth (or possibly from Athens) in the middle of the journey to Greece described in Acts.

The evidence of 1 Thessalonians

How does the evidence of 1 Thessalonians fit with what we have seen in Acts?

- We have noted that the general picture of the various movements of Paul, Silas and Timothy between Thessalonica and Athens and Corinth is confirmed.
- Their previous ministry in Philippi is also alluded to (2.1), and Paul's comment on how they had 'suffered and been insulted in Philippi' fits with the Acts story of Paul and Silas being in prison and then confronted by the authorities. As for Paul and

Silas being flogged and put in prison, Paul's later letter of 2 Corinthians refers to such experiences, though not explicitly relating them to Philippi (11.23).

- 1 Thessalonians confirms that there was major trouble in Thessalonica, involving not just Paul and his companions but the Thessalonian Christians (1.6). Paul mentions their sufferings as similar to the sufferings inflicted on the churches in Judaea by the Jews, and Paul speaks with some bitterness of the Jews, in a way that makes sense if they were his particular opponents in Thessalonica, which is what Acts indicates (Acts 17.5ff.; cf. 1 Thessalonians 2.15: 'they displease God and are hostile to all men, in their effort to keep us from speaking to the Gentiles').
- Acts describes Paul preaching in the synagogue for three sabbaths, and it could be assumed that he was only in Thessalonica for three or four weeks. 1 Thessalonians suggests a longer ministry. However, there is not necessarily any major disagreement here: Acts may not be implying that Paul was only in Thessalonica for four weeks, and 1 Thessalonians suggests that Paul left the Thessalonian church in a young and vulnerable state.
- Paul speaks of his gentle ministry among the Thessalonians, and of how we 'toiled night and day in order not to be a burden to anyone while we preached the gospel of God to you' (2.6–9). The references here to his hard work, and to working with his hands in 4.11, are interesting: Acts mentions Paul's tent-making in Corinth (in collaboration with Aquila and Priscilla), and so confirms that this was his practice on this missionary journey.

Paul's preaching to the Thessalonians

Particularly intriguing is the evidence of 1 Thessalonians on how and what Paul preached to the Greeks. In 1 Thessalonians 1.9–10 Paul speaks of how the Thessalonians were converted: 'You turned to God from idols to serve the living and true God, and to wait for his Son from heaven, whom he raised from the dead – Jesus, who rescues us from the coming wrath.' What is interesting is how similar this short summary statement is to Paul's speech to the Areopagus described in Acts 17. In both we notice:

- a contrasting of idols with the living and true God
  - 1 Thessalonians 1.9: 'you turned to God from idols to serve the living and true God'
  - Acts 17.22–29: 'in him we live and move and have our being [. . .] we should not think that the divine being is like gold or silver or stone – an image'
- the theme of repenting from idolatry
  - 1 Thessalonians 1.9: 'you turned to God from idols'
  - Acts 17.30: 'now he commands all people everywhere to repent'
- a reference to coming judgement
  - 1 Thessalonians 1.10: 'to wait for his Son from heaven . . . Jesus who rescues us from the coming wrath'
  - Acts 17.31: 'for he has set a day when he will judge the world'
- the connecting of this coming judgement with Jesus' resurrection
  - 1 Thessalonians 1.10: 'to wait for his Son from heaven, whom he raised from the dead, Jesus'
  - Acts 17.31: 'he will judge the world by the man he has appointed; he has given proof of this to all men by raising him from the dead'

These parallels suggest that Acts accurately describes how Paul preached during this missionary journey in Greece. In 1 Thessalonians he is writing about his ministry to the Thessalonians, which took place just before he went to Athens, and he is writing from Corinth, just after he had been in Athens. It is, therefore, entirely probable that in Athens he will have preached and ministered in the sort of way described in 1 Thessalonians 1.9–10, as Acts also suggests.

I put this point strongly, because scholars have often doubted whether Acts 17 does represent Paul's preaching, claiming that its emphases and approach are contrary to the Paul we know from elsewhere. Paul in Acts 17 does not preach directly about Jesus and the cross, but takes a more roundabout approach, talking about creation and idolatry and bringing in quotations from Greek poets. According to some this is not the real Paul. But 1 Thessalonians, written just after his stay in Athens, about his ministry immediately before he came to Athens, disproves this claim decisively, and suggests that when preaching to Greeks and Gentiles Paul started where they were (as indeed he does when he preaches in the synagogue, starting there with the Old Testament; compare Paul's remarks in 1 Corinthians 9.20–1 about being a Jew to Jews and a Greek to Greeks, in order to win them for Christ).

Some scholars have dismissed the significance of the parallels between Acts 17 and 1 Thessalonians 1, suggesting that this was simply a typical Jewish or Christian approach to Gentiles – so that the similarity is coincidental. But that viewpoint is an admission that this might well have been Paul's approach, and it seems distinctly perverse to claim that Acts was describing a typical form of preaching, when the author obviously does know about Paul's visit to Athens and when other evidence suggests that this is just how Paul will have preached.

What is the 'wrath'?

One final piece of evidence relating to 1 Thessalonians and Acts concerns the much-discussed and difficult verse 1 Thessalonians 2.16, where Paul says of the Jews that 'the wrath of God has come on them at last'. Scholars have been very puzzled by this statement, and some have argued that it must be a comment by a scribe writing after the terrible destruction of Jerusalem by the Romans in AD 70.

However, Acts suggests an alternative possibility. Acts tells us that Paul stayed in Corinth with Priscilla and Aquila, who had come from Rome after the great expulsion of the Jews by the emperor Claudius in AD 49. If Paul wrote 1 Thessalonians at precisely this time, as we have suggested, then could it be that Paul's reference to the 'wrath' visited on the Jews is a reference to the emperor's action? In favour of this is the following:

1. The timing would fit.
2. Living with Aquila and Priscilla, Paul must have had the expulsion very much in his mind.
3. Paul's comment about the 'wrath' coming on the Jews follows some very strong words about opposition to the Christians from 'the Jews', who 'displease God and are hostile to all men in their effort to keep us from speaking to the Gentiles so that they may be saved' (2.15–16). If, as we suggested earlier, the

troubles in Rome were like other troubles between Jews and Christians, then they will have been provoked by the divisive impact of the Christian mission on the Jewish community. Some Jews (like Aquila and Priscilla) became Christians and started to propagate the Christian message, perhaps even among 'unclean' Gentiles; others tried to hold the line against this novel interpretation. If this was the historical context, then Paul's strong words about Jewish opposition to the gospel make sense (though Paul has in mind not just what happened in Rome, but also what had happened in Judaea, Thessalonica and elsewhere); it also makes sense to see Paul's comments on the 'wrath' coming on the Jews as a reference to the expulsion from Rome.

Admittedly, the 'wrath' may perhaps seem to us an odd way to refer to the Roman expulsion of the Jews. The reference is probably to divine wrath, not just to the emperor's wrath (see 1.10). But to anyone knowing the Old Testament, God's wrath more than anything else would suggest some sort of natural, political or military disaster, often at the hands of powerful pagan enemies (2 Chronicles 24.18; Jeremiah 32.37; Ezekiel 7.19; Zechariah 7.12; etc.); the sending of the Jews into exile was a prime example of God's wrath in the Old Testament. The expulsion of the Jews from Rome would fit into that category rather well.

If it still sounds rather strong language to us, three further things are worth saying:

1. Paul uses precisely the same word, 'wrath', in Romans 13.4–5 of punishment meted out by the Roman state.
2. For the Jews affected by the expulsion it will have been a traumatic experience. As we have seen, there was a large Jewish community in Rome, and for them to have the emperor turn against them will not only have been highly inconvenient and probably disastrous for many Jewish individuals and families in Rome, but also very alarming for Jews throughout the world, given that there was plenty of anti-Semitism in the Roman world.
3. And this was not the only disaster to hit the Jews at this time: there was a whole series of unhappy events. Most notably,

Josephus the Jewish historian tells us that between 20 and 30 thousand Jews were killed in Jerusalem in the year AD 49. The context was a riot and stampede provoked by a Roman soldier who infuriated the Jews by displaying his backside and farting deliberately in full public view in the temple area (*Antiquities* II, 223–7). Even if Josephus's numbers are exaggerated, it is clear that it was a disaster on a massive scale.

It would have been natural enough to see this catastrophe and the expulsion from Rome – both events involving Jews and Romans, one in Rome and one in Jerusalem – as a divine double blow against the Jews.

If the suggestion about the 'wrath' and the expulsion of the Jews from Rome is correct, then it not only throws light on a perplexing phrase in 1 Thessalonians, but is also a striking convergence between Acts and Paul's letters. Even if that suggestion is not correct, the other evidence we have looked at in Paul's letters, notably in 1 Thessalonians, tends to confirm the account of Paul's ministry that we find in the book of Acts.

NOTE ON THE EXPULSION FROM ROME

In support of the idea that the 'wrath' in 1 Thessalonians 2 could refer to Claudius's edict, it may be worth mentioning that the edict and its effects have been seen to lie behind Paul's letter to the Romans.

Romans is arguably, more than anything else, a plea to Jewish Christians and Gentile Christians to live harmoniously together. This comes out most clearly in chapters 14 and 15, for example in 15.7–8, where Paul says: 'Accept one another, then, just as Christ accepted you, in order to bring praise to God. For I tell you that Christ has become a servant of *the Jews* on behalf of God's truth, to confirm the promises made to the patriarchs, so that *the Gentiles* may glorify God for his mercy'. It has been suggested by various scholars that the historical background to this emphasis in Romans may be the expulsion of Jews from Rome.

If, as seems probable, the Christian church in Rome was first a Jewish Christian church, perhaps led by people such as Aquila and Priscilla, this presumably changed suddenly when the Jews and the Jewish Christians (especially their leaders, no doubt) were expelled from Rome. Gentile Christians will likely have come to the fore, and there may have been a tendency among the Gentile Christians to see the Jews as has-beens and even as under 'the wrath' of God. Paul, to the contrary, warns Gentile Christians not to gloat over the Jews (Romans 11.22–4).

But after the death of Claudius in AD 54, the Jews were able to return to Rome, and so were the Jewish Christian leaders like Aquila and Priscilla. By the time Romans was written, they are back in Rome (16.3), and so were other Jewish Christians (see v. 7 and perhaps v. 13, if Rufus and his mother are rightly regarded as connected with Simon of Cyrene: see Mark 15.21). It is not difficult to imagine the tensions that may have arisen when the Jewish Christian leaders and members came back, and it may well be that Romans was written with that particularly in mind: Romans is a sustained and brilliant explanation of the relationship between the Old Testament and the Jews on the one hand, and the new way of Christ and the Gentiles on the other.

This interpretation of Romans does not directly support the book of Acts, but it fits in with what Acts says about the expulsion and about Aquila and Priscilla, and with what we have suggested about 1 Thessalonians and the 'wrath'. It is another case of Paul's letters and the book of Acts casting light on each other.

9 What is going on in 1 Thessalonians?

A sigh of relief

'Timothy has just now come to us from you and has brought good news about your faith and love. He has told us that you always have pleasant memories of us and that you long to see us, just as we also long to see you' (1 Thessalonians 3.6). This verse puts Paul's first letter to the Thessalonians into its context; the letter is something like a giant sigh of relief.

He has been very anxious for the Thessalonian Christians, having founded the church there, but having had to leave these young Christians because of fierce and violent opposition. Not surprisingly he was anxious for his children in the faith, hoping that they were surviving, hoping that their faith had not been shaken. He had wanted to return to them, 'but Satan stopped us' (2.18); presumably it just wasn't safe. So, when he could bear the suspense no longer, Paul sent Timothy to find out how they were. Now Timothy has returned, with good news.

The first three chapters of 1 Thessalonians – more than half of the letter – are Paul's thankful sigh of relief. Whereas in Galatians there was no opening thanksgiving, but a cry of pain at the Galatians' fall from faith, in 1 Thessalonians Paul starts joyfully with the words: 'We always thank God for all of you' (1.2). He goes on to speak of their faith, love and hope (1.3), and then recalls their conversion (1.4–10), his ministry among them (2.1–13), their sufferings (2.14–16), his forcible separation from them and his subsequent anxiety for their welfare (2.17—3.5). But now Timothy has come, and Paul is overjoyed: 'For now we really live, since you are standing firm in the Lord. How can we thank God enough for you in return for all the joy we have in the presence of our God because of you?' (3.8–9).

Paul's deep affection for his converts is clear in Galatians, though the affection there is mixed with anger and pain at how they have been seduced. 1 Thessalonians is an equally emotional letter, but this time it is a case of deep affection mixed with initial anxiety and subsequent relief and great happiness. We get a powerful picture of Paul as a pastor, seeking to act with integrity (2.3–4), caring for his people with gentleness and giving himself to them, like a loving mother or father (2.7, 11). Paul is no nine-to-five professional, but someone totally committed to those among whom he works and has worked. He comments: 'You are our glory and our joy' (2.20).

Issues raised by Timothy

Timothy no doubt discussed with Paul everything that was going on in the Thessalonian church. It is not difficult to imagine the eager catching-up on news when his young assistant came to Paul in Corinth. Although the most important item was the good news of their steadfastness in faith, all sorts of other issues were being faced by the Thessalonians. And we may assume that these influenced the second half of Paul's letter: he urges sexual self-control and brotherly love – advice still needed in most churches!

Hard work and Christian sharing

Paul urges the Thessalonians to 'mind their own business and to work with your hands ... so that your daily life may win the respect of outsiders and so that you will not be dependent on anybody' (4.11, 12). It sounds as though some of the Thessalonians may have been opting out and living off the generosity of others. The book of Acts suggests that the earliest Christians had a very strong community life, the rich (like Barnabas) sharing their wealth with the poor (Acts 4.32–7). Did Barnabas and his colleague Paul encourage this in the churches that they founded? Certainly they encouraged such sharing between churches, and Paul in 2 Corinthians 8–10, when organizing a major collection among the Gentile churches, expresses his belief in generous sharing and in equality. Such generosity is always open to abuse (as governments with welfare programmes know well), and it may be that some in Thessalonica were abusing the 'brotherly love' which Paul has just advocated.

The Lord's return and those who have died

But the big issue in Thessalonica seems to have been connected with their understanding of the second coming of Jesus. It is quite clear that a key element in their faith was their expectation of Jesus' imminent return. Thus in speaking of their conversion Paul comments on how they turned to serve the living and true God 'and to wait for his Son from heaven ... Jesus, who rescues us from the coming wrath' (1.9, 10). Paul does not criticize this expectation; indeed in the conclusion to the letter he prays for the Thessalonians to be kept blameless 'at the coming of our Lord Jesus Christ' (5.23).

It is significant that at the end of his later letter of 1 Corinthians Paul writes the Aramaic word 'Maranatha' (16.22). We might wonder what this Aramaic word is doing there, popping up with no explanation at the end of a letter written in Greek. The answer is that the word means 'Our Lord come' (or 'Our Lord comes'), and that it must have been a particularly important part of the early Christians' prayers – hence its survival in Aramaic even within Greek-speaking churches. The early Christians were eagerly awaiting the return of their Lord who, after all, had only been gone for twenty years and who had promised to return.

If the Corinthians prayed 'Maranatha', we may guess that the Thessalonians, whose church was founded by Paul shortly before the Corinthian church, will have done so too. But, whether or not they did, they were evidently full of anticipation of the Lord's return. It is probably not a coincidence that they were a church under pressure: in times of persecution the promise that the Lord will return to save his people is especially important (as the book of Revelation also shows). It is interesting that in Galatians the Lord's return seems not to have been an issue at all; the issue was the question of the Jewish law, because of the Jewish Christians' campaign to get the Gentile Christians circumcised and integrated into Judaism. In 1 Thessalonians there is no hint that Jewish Christians have appeared on the scene – Paul has after all only recently left Thessalonica. The problem in Thessalonica is not Jewish Christian infiltration of the church, but rather Jewish persecution of Christians. In that context the good news of the Lord's return is especially important.

But what was the problem with the Thessalonians' beliefs? The answer is that they were getting upset at the death of some of their Christian brothers and sisters (4.13). Apparently they feared that

93

those who had died would miss out in some way on the Lord's return and on all the blessings that this would bring.

Their anxieties may seem odd to us, looking back after two millennia of Christians passing away. But they are not at all so odd, given that:

- Jesus had been around only twenty years previously;
- they were expecting him to come back any time;
- they were looking forward to being with him in his 'kingdom and glory' (2.12) and to deliverance from their present sufferings;
- relatively few Christians had died thus far, especially in Thessalonica, where the church had just been founded!

It is understandable that they may have concluded, sadly, that those who died before the Lord's return must have missed out on the blessings he was going to bring.

The Thessalonian problem highlights both the importance of the second coming to the first Christians (a contrast to much modern Christianity) and the fact that they were expecting him to come soon, not in the distant future.

In response to their grief over their dead loved ones, Paul reminds them of Jesus' resurrection from the dead, assures them that those who 'fall asleep' as Christians – 'in' Jesus – will share his resurrection, and tells them that, far from missing out or even being consigned to second place when the Lord returns, the Christian dead will rise first, and then Christians who are alive will join them to meet the returning Lord (4.13–18).

Clearly one of the questions raised by all of this is the time of the Lord's coming, and so Paul then goes on to remind them of what they know 'very well' about the Lord coming like a thief in the night, and about the need to be prepared – living in the light and being spiritually armed with faith, hope and love (5.1–8).

Questions of leadership

Paul's letter concludes with a variety of brief exhortations. It is interesting that he urges the Thessalonians 'to respect those who work hard among you, who are over you in the Lord and who admonish you. Hold them in highest regard because of their work'

(1 Thessalonians 5.12–13). This suggests that there were recognized leaders in the church, though they are not mentioned earlier in the letter. Acts describes Paul and Barnabas appointing 'elders' in the churches which they established in Galatia (14.23). Some scholars have suspected Acts of reading back later church order into his account of events, but 1 Thessalonians, though describing Paul's next missionary journey, lends support to Acts. It is in any case totally improbable that Paul and his team would have left the churches they founded without any organized leadership. It is true, and significant, that there is no sign in Paul's letters of the sort of top-heavy clericalism that has been a feature of the Christian church so often in history; but there are recognized leaders – in 1 Thessalonians and also in Galatians, where Paul urges Christians to support those who teach the church (6.6).

The Holy Spirit

One final point to note in 1 Thessalonians is in 5.19: 'Do not put out the Spirit's fire; do not treat prophecies with contempt. Test everything.' Although we should not read too much into such brief exhortations, we may reasonably conclude that the Thessalonian church was, to some extent at least, a charismatic church, and that prophets played a part in its life. This is only what we would expect from what we have seen of Paul's ministry so far. But the form of the exhortation may imply that there was some controversy about the prophetic ministry, and perhaps some hostility to it. We will see later on how important these issues were in the Thessalonians' sister church in Corinth.

10 What does 1 Thessalonians tell us about Paul and Jesus?

We have looked at what is going on in 1 Thessalonians. But now is the time to return to our detective work, and to try to work out, as we did earlier with Galatians, something of what lies behind Paul's teaching in the letter. Where do the ideas that he expresses in the letter come from? Clearly a lot of what he says is his immediate response to recent events: Paul is expressing his feelings of anxiety and then joy. But are there clues as to what he had taught the Thessalonians before? And, in particular, can we detect knowledge of Jesus and of his teaching?

The Lord's future coming

The most concentrated teaching in 1 Thessalonians is to do with the future and Jesus' return. We have already seen that the church members were anxious about their loved ones who had died: this anxiety probably reflects the fact that they were looking forward not to life after death in heaven, but to Jesus coming back before they died and establishing the kingdom of God. Where did they get their ideas from?

The answer must be that they got their ideas from Paul and his team (even if they did not entirely get Paul's meaning, as it turns out). Paul had taught them about the returning Lord; that was part of the gospel he preached to them (1.10, 5.1–11).

But where did Paul get his beliefs about Jesus' return from? He would not obviously or necessarily have learned this aspect of his faith through his Damascus Road experience 'by revelation'. More likely he learned it from the Church which regularly prayed 'Maranatha'; in particular there is reason to think that he knew Jesus' teaching on the matter.

There is a large amount of teaching of Jesus in the gospels on the subject of the future. For example, there is the long 'eschatological

96

discourse', where Jesus speaks of future sufferings, including the destruction of the Jerusalem temple and the 'desolation' of the temple, and then of the coming of the Son of Man on the clouds and of the need to be awake for that day (Mark 13; Matthew 24; Luke 21; cf. also Luke 17); there are also numerous parables about being ready for the coming of the absent Lord (e.g. the parables of the thief, the doorkeeper(s), the steward, the wise and foolish virgins, the talents: Matthew 24.42—25.30; Luke 12.35–48).

The evidence for Paul's familiarity with this teaching is extensive.

The thief in the night

A good starting point is his reference in 1 Thessalonians to the day of the Lord coming like a thief in the night (5.2), since this inevitably reminds us of Jesus' parable of the thief. Paul could in theory have come up himself with this striking picture of the Lord's coming, and the gospel writers, in theory, could have got the idea from Paul, not from the teaching of Jesus. However, there are all sorts of things that make these theoretical possibilities unlikely.

1. Matthew and Luke, who record the parable, say that it came from Jesus!
2. It is most unlikely that any Christians would have compared their master Jesus to a thief! Jewish tradition did not speak of the coming day of the Lord. The only person in that way likely to have compared Jesus' coming to that of a thief is Jesus himself.
3. Paul says that the Thessalonians 'know very well' that the day of the Lord will come like a thief, suggesting that this was a well-known tradition, such as might well have come from Jesus.
4. There is evidence of Paul echoing other parables of Jesus in the same context in 1 Thessalonians, as we shall see.

The word of the Lord

Further evidence of Paul's familiarity with Jesus' teaching is his comment that he has a 'word from the Lord' relevant to the Thessalonians' anxieties about their fellow Christians who have 'fallen asleep' before the Lord's return (4.15). He assures them that those who are alive will not precede those who have died, and he proceeds to describe how 'the Lord himself will come down from heaven with a loud command, with the voice of the archangel and with the trumpet call of God, and the dead in Chrst will rise first. After that, we who are still alive and are left will be caught up together with them in the clouds to meet the Lord in the air. And so we will be with the Lord for ever' (4.15–17).

What did Paul mean when he said that he had 'a word from the Lord' relevant to the Thessalonians? Did he simply mean that he himself felt led by the Lord to say what he says? It sounds something rather more than that. Was he referring to a prophecy that he had had or heard? We know that prophecy was important to him. Or was he referring to the teaching of Jesus?

In favour of this last possibility is the similarity of what Paul says to the teaching of Jesus. Jesus in Matthew, Mark and Luke speaks of his coming as the Son of man on the clouds of heaven, to save his people (Matthew 24.30–1; Mark 13.26–7; Luke 21.27–8); in Matthew and Mark he speaks of coming with the angels, and of sending them to gather God's elect from 'the ends of the earth to the ends of the heavens'. In Matthew there is a reference to a loud trumpet blast (24.31). Given this evidence, the obvious conclusion is that Paul is drawing on the teaching of Jesus; that is his 'word from the Lord'.

Of course, 'obvious' conclusions are not always correct, and it is possible to argue that since Matthew's trumpet, for example, is not in Mark, which is usually seen as the earliest gospel, it may be Matthew's addition to Mark, not an original word of Jesus. It is even possible that Matthew was influenced by Paul, or that they both got the idea of the trumpet from Old Testament descriptions of the day of the Lord (e.g. Isaiah 27.13). However, although these things are possible, the simpler explanation is that Matthew, who certainly had other sources of information about Jesus than Mark, and Paul both knew the same 'word of the Lord'.

But there is another possible problem: Paul implies that his 'word of the Lord' somehow addresses the question of Christians who have 'fallen asleep', whereas the teaching of Jesus about the Son of Man coming on the clouds says nothing about those who are dead. Paul might have deduced that the angels in gathering the elect would have included the dead, but that is not explicit. So is 'the word of the Lord' after all more likely to be a prophecy?

98

A different possibility is that Paul knew Jesus' parable of the wise and the foolish virgins (Matthew 25.1–13). It describes ten girls, each with a lamp, waiting for the bridegroom to arrive for the wedding; the bridegroom is seriously delayed, and the girls fall asleep while waiting. When eventually the bridegroom comes at midnight, the girls find that the oil for their lamps has run out; but five have spare oil with them, and therefore go to the wedding. The other five have to go and buy oil, and miss out on the feast and celebration. In the context in Matthew the parable is clearly about Jesus' return, and about the need to be ready for his coming. But what is interesting from the point of view of Paul is that it speaks of people who have fallen asleep going to the wedding feast. Was this Paul's 'word of the Lord', on the basis of which he assured the Thessalonians that their deceased loved ones were not lost?

That may sound like unlikely logic to us. Isn't it a big leap from the parable about girls falling literally asleep to conclusions about Christians who have died? We might think so, but three observations are relevant:

- Seeing death as 'sleep' seems to have been characteristic of the early Christians, and the gospels suggest that this goes back to Jesus (e.g. Mark 5.39; John 11.11). This does not mean that the parable of the virgins necessarily had anything to do with death, but it helps us see why Paul might have made the connection.

- Although the parable need not be seen as having anything to do with death, it could have been seen as precisely relevant to the Thessalonians' situation, since it describes a situation of the awaited master coming later than expected and indeed a situation of people unable to keep awake until his coming. The parable thus lent itself to Paul's purpose. Admittedly some scholars argue that parables like this, which speak of the delay of the Lord's coming, cannot come from Jesus himself, but must come from a later time when the delay of the Lord's return became a problem. However, that view is debatable to say the least, and the gospel evidence is that Jesus taught that the time of his return was unknown: it could be earlier than anticipated, as in his parable of the unprepared steward who

99

mistreated his fellow servants and was caught out (Matthew 24.45–51), or it could be later, as in the parable of the virgins.

- The decisive evidence in favour of identifying Paul's 'word of the Lord' with the parable is linguistic, since his description of the Lord's coming has significant resemblances to Jesus' parable:

 (a) he speaks of the 'Lord' coming; the foolish virgins address the bridegroom as 'lord, lord';

 (b) he speaks of the Lord coming with a loud command; the bridegroom is announced with a 'cry [...] come out to meet him';

 (c) he speaks of us being caught up with those who have fallen asleep 'to meet' the Lord in the air; the virgins are summoned 'to meet' him. The Greek for 'to meet' (*eis apantesin*) is a somewhat unusual phrase, at least within the New Testament, but identical in 1 Thessalonans and the parable in Matthew;

 (d) he speaks of people who have fallen asleep before the master's coming 'rising' to meet him; the virgins 'arose' and trimmed their lamps, though only some were ready;

 (e) he speaks of Christians finally 'being with the Lord for ever'; the wise virgins go into the wedding 'with him'.

This all adds up to rather strong evidence for Paul's knowledge of Jesus' parable, especially given the reference to 'the word of the Lord' and the other parallels to Jesus' teaching (about the coming of the Son of Man) in the same passage. And we should add also our earlier observation that Paul knows the parable of the thief, which is almost adjacent to that of the virgins in Matthew.

If Paul knew these two eschatological parables of Jesus, did he know others? Mark and Luke record a parable of Jesus about one or more watchmen who are left by a master to guard the door of his house at night; the message of that parable, namely 'keep awake, don't fall asleep', is rather different from that of the virgins (Mark 13.33–4; Luke 12.36–7). Paul could well be echoing that in 1 Thessalonians 4 and 5, especially 5.6: 'So let us not be like others, who are asleep, but let us be alert and self-controlled'. As for Jesus' parable of the steward, that may well be echoed by Paul in 1

Corinthians 4.1–5, where Paul says that he and Apollos are trusted servants of Christ, who will have to give account when he comes.

In making these comparisons, we need to be careful of 'parallelomania', as someone has called it, when scholars find similar things or ideas and think that there must be a significant link. The detective must be careful not to get too excited by a particular theory and then read everything that way. With respect to the evidence we have been examining, it could be objected that we have been finding all sorts of links, but that some are with Matthew's gospel, some with Mark's, some with Luke's; this sounds like an unscientific pick-and-mix. After all, the parable of the virgins is only in Matthew's gospel – it is not in Mark and Luke; so is it likely that Paul will have known it? The parable of the thief is in Matthew and Luke, but not Mark; how is it that Paul has it and Mark doesn't? The parable of the watchman at the door is not in Matthew, but only Mark and Luke.

These observations and warnings are valid, but they do not undermine the case. After all, Paul's letters were presumably written before any of the gospels, and so he wasn't picking-and-mixing from our gospels. He was drawing on the teaching of Jesus, which the gospel writers also drew on. In fact the gospel writers and Paul were all doing something of a pick-and-mix from Jesus' teaching. Quite apart from Paul's evidence, there is weighty evidence for the view that Matthew, Mark and Luke all knew various parables of Jesus about his future coming from which they only chose some. Luke knew the parable of the virgins, but only records a phrase from it (Luke 12.35); Matthew knew the parable of the watchman, but likewise only has a phrase from it (Matthew 24.42); Mark knew several of the parables, but only alludes to them briefly (Mark 13.33–7). However, we cannot investigate that evidence in this book (but see my earlier book, *Paul: Follower of Jesus or Founder of Christianity?* for fuller discussion); from our point of view at the moment what is important is the strong evidence of Paul's knowledge of Jesus' teaching about the Lord's return, and the strong evidence that Jesus' teaching had been passed on to the Thessalonians. The Thessalonians' eager expectation of the Lord's return derived, so it seems, not from some curious aberration in their own thinking, nor from general teaching from Paul that 'the day of the

Lord will come', but from Jesus' own description of his return in glory and his vivid parables about the returning master.

The judgement of the Jews

In Matthew 24, Mark 13 and Luke 21 the teaching of Jesus about his future coming is preceded by dire warnings of a catastrophe that is going to come on Jerusalem, 'in this generation'. Did Paul know this teaching? The evidence from 1 Thessalonians that may point in that direction is the reference in 2.16 to the 'wrath' having come on the Jews.

We have noticed how scholars have been perplexed by this verse: they have found it difficult to make sense of, and some have argued that the whole passage, where Paul speaks with untypical fierceness about the Jews – 'they displease God and are hostile to all men' – does not actually come from Paul, but from a scribe writing, quite probably, after the destruction of Jerusalem in AD 70. We have, however, argued that the events of AD 49, namely the expulsion of the Jews from Rome and the slaughter of the Jews in Jerusalem, make very good sense of Paul's reference to the 'wrath' coming on the Jews, and fit exactly into the historical context of the letter.

But there remains an unanswered question: why does Paul speak of the events so indirectly and briefly as 'the wrath', which 'has come on them at last'? What sense would that have made to the Thessalonians? Or was Paul just mumbling theologically to himself?! A possible answer is suggested by the gospels' account of Jesus' teaching: if Paul knew and had passed on to the Thessalonians the teaching of Jesus about the future, as we have already argued, and if that teaching included Jesus' warnings about judgement coming on Jerusalem and the Jews, then his allusion to wrath coming on the Jews would have made perfect sense. They were expecting something terrible to happen to the Jewish nation in the near future, and sure enough now it seemed to be happening, thanks to Claudius and others.

This answer can be supported in various ways.

First, the future disaster coming on Jerusalem as described by Jesus in the gospels would very likely have been associated with the Romans. When Jesus spoke of the future destruction of Jerusalem, the Romans were the only obvious threat. When Jesus spoke of the temple being desecrated, the people most likely to do that were the Romans.

The phrase by Jesus used in Matthew and Mark is 'the abomination of desolation' (or 'the desolating sacrilege'), and it is a phrase that for Jesus and his Jewish contemporaries recalled the terrible events in 167 BC, when the then-powerful Syrian ruler, Antiochus IV Epiphanes, invaded the temple, turned it over to pagan worship, and tried to abolish the practice of the Jewish religion by force. Fortunately, and thanks to the courageous resistance of the famous family of the Maccabees, the abomination only lasted for three years, but for the Jews ever afterwards this was the horror that they feared and that must never happen again. When Pontius Pilate, after his appointment as governor of Judaea in AD 26, ordered his troops to enter Jerusalem with their military standards, there was a huge popular protest at this desecration of the Holy City; eventually Pilate was forced to back down.

It is easy to see, therefore, that when Jesus spoke of the future desolation of Jerusalem, people will have associated this with the Romans and the threat they represented. And when in AD 49 the Roman emperor acted so drastically against the Jews in Rome, and a Roman soldier provoked a disastrous riot by his indecency in the vicinity of the temple, it is easy to see how this could have been regarded as the beginning of what Jesus had promised. (We might think, looking back, that it was a mistaken interpretation: the destruction of Jerusalem was not to happen until AD 70. But then we have the advantage of hindsight. And in fact it is not so fanciful to see the events of AD 49 as an important moment in the lead-up to the Jewish war of AD 66–70).

Second, Luke actually describes the coming disaster somewhat differently from Matthew and Mark, but interestingly he speaks of it as 'wrath [coming] on this people' (21.23). In other words, the very word and thought that is found in 1 Thessalonians 2.16 is in the Lukan version of Jesus' eschatological teaching. The explanation, therefore, that offers itself of Paul's use of the term 'wrath' is that it came from the teaching of Jesus.

A difficulty with this view may be that the word is in Luke and not in Matthew and Mark, and many scholars think that Luke's version is a rewriting of Mark; so the word may not go back to Jesus. That view may be correct: Luke may have rewritten the teaching to make it more intelligible to his Gentile readers, thus replacing the mysterious phrase 'abomination of desolation' with a more straightforward reference to Jersualem being attacked by Gentile armies. However, it has not at all been proved that Luke is entirely or even primarily dependent on Mark here, and it could be that he has another version, which was also known to Paul. But even if Luke's version is a rewriting of Mark, Luke is still of great interest, because it shows that someone in the Pauline circle, as the author of Luke–Acts seems to be, interprets the teaching of Jesus about the catastrophe coming on Jerusalem as 'wrath' on the Jews. In other words, Luke shows that our suggestion that Paul saw the Roman actions against the Jews as the judgement promised by Jesus makes good sense.

Third, there is other evidence that Paul is echoing the teaching of Jesus in 1 Thessalonians 2.13–16. In verse 16 itself, where he speaks of the 'wrath' coming on the Jews 'at last', the Greek for 'at last' is *eis telos*, which is perhaps more naturally translated 'to the end'. But what would 'to the end' mean in this context? What is interesting is that the phrase is used in the Matthew/Mark form of Jesus' teaching immediately before the description of the 'abomination of desolation' (Matthew 24.13; Mark 13.13). Jesus speaks there of the disciples engaging in mission 'to the Gentiles' and of them facing great persecution and suffering; in that context the promise is that 'he who endures to the end' will be saved. Paul in 1 Thessalonians 2.14–16 is talking about suffering, preaching to the Gentiles, and people being 'saved', and it is by no means impossible that the phrase 'to the end' comes from that teaching of Jesus.

Something similar may be said about Paul's references in that passage to the Jews 'who killed the Lord Jesus and the prophets and also drove us out. [. . .] so as to fill up sins always. The wrath of God has come upon them at last' (2.15, 16). The comparison in this case is with Matthew 23.29–36 (which has a partial parallel in Luke 11.47–51), where Jesus speaks against the scribes and Pharisees, accusing them of following in their forefathers' footsteps and killing the prophets. Jesus comments, 'Fill up the measure of your fathers' (23.32); he goes on to speak of how they 'kill', 'crucify', and 'pursue [or 'drive'] from city to city' those sent to them, and of how the righteous blood of God's messengers will be required of them: 'Truly I say to you, all these things will come on this generation' (23.36). The similar combination of ideas in Paul and Matthew is interesting at least – both have the ideas of driving out and killing the prophets and messengers of God, of somehow 'filling up' the measure of their sins, and the promise of divine judgement soon.

Some scholars have commented that the language of 1 Thessalonians 2.14–16 is not typically Pauline. That sort of scholarly judgement is usually precarious but, if there is anything in it in this case, then it could be that we have in these verses not just Paul himself speaking with particular passion after what he and the Thessalonians have been through, but also him echoing, consciously or unconsciously, various of the teachings of Jesus relating to future sufferings and salvation.

Fourth, there is a bit of evidence elsewhere in Paul's letters for his being familiar with the version of Jesus' teaching about the future attested in Luke. Thus, in 1 Corinthians 7.26 Paul speaks of the 'present crisis/distress' as a reason for the unmarried to remain single. The Greek word for 'crisis/distress' here is *anangke*, which is exactly the same word as is used in Luke 21.23, where Jesus says that 'there will be great distress on the earth' (or 'in the land'); this is immediately before Jesus' saying about 'wrath' coming on the Jews – thus 'there will be great distress on the earth and wrath on this people'. If in 1 Thessalonians 2.16 Paul could speak about 'the wrath' and have in mind the disasters that struck the Jews in AD 49, here in 1 Corinthians he could be referring to the terrible famine that hit the Roman world at about the time he was writing 1 Corinthians, seeing that as a sign that 'the time is short' before the Lord's return (as he says a few verses later, in 7.29).

Then there is Romans 11, where Paul is concluding a long discussion of the Jews' unbelief and failure to come into the Church. He sees them as under God's wrath at present, hence their hard hearts (cf. 9.22); but he says: 'a hardening has come on part of Israel until the fulness of the Gentiles come in, and so all Israel will be saved' (11.25). This is intriguingly similar to Luke 21, where Paul talks about wrath on the Jewish nation and about Jerusalem being 'trampled under foot by Gentiles, until the times of the Gentiles are fulfilled' (v. 24). The ideas are not identical – in Romans there is no reference to Jerusalem being invaded or trampled on – but there is a broad parallel between the passages, which could point to Paul's familiarity with the relevant teaching of Jesus.

Fifth, when we move to 2 Thessalonians, we will see that there is strong evidence there for Paul's having taught the Thessalonians about the 'abomination of desolation'. But we will look at this, and at the question of whether 2 Thessalonians is a genuine letter of Paul, in the next chapter.

The suddenness of the Lord's coming

We have seen various echoes of Matthew 24, Mark 13 and Luke 21 in 1 Thessalonians. One other is 1 Thessalonians 5.2–3, where Paul speaks of the day of the Lord coming like a thief (as we have seen), and then continues, 'when people are saying "Peace and safety", destruction will come on them suddenly, like labour pains on a pregnant woman, and they will not escape.' Paul goes on in the following verses to urge wakefulness and sobriety, as opposed to drunkenness.

Some scholars have again argued that the phraseology in 1 Thessalonians 5.3 in particular is not typical of Paul, but it does have interesting parallels in Luke 21.34–6, where Jesus ends his teaching about the future with these words: 'Be careful, or your hearts will be weighed down with dissipation, drunkenness and the anxieties of life, and that day will come on you suddenly like a trap. For it will come upon all those who live on the face of the whole earth. Be always awake, and pray that you may be able to escape all that is about to happen, and that you may be able to stand before the Son of Man.'

The general similarity of thought in the two passages is clear enough, but there are particularly striking verbal links as well, notably these:

- the same word for 'suddenly', a Greek word never used elsewhere in the New Testament;
- the same word for 'come on' (not a usual word in Paul's letters);

- the reference to 'escaping' in the context of judgement;
- the comparison of the coming day to something sudden: in 1 Thessalonians it is 'like a trap', in Luke it is 'like labour pains'. Admittedly these are rather different things (even if parents do sometimes feel trapped after childbirth!), but there is one Hebrew-Aramaic word, which Jesus could have used, and which can be translated in both ways.

Whether or not the last point is significant, the other similarities are impressive, and we may suspect that Luke and Paul are connected. We saw earlier how Paul can be linked with the distinctively Lukan description of the 'wrath' coming on Jerusalem; we seem now to have another case of Lukan eschatological material being known to Paul. This particular case may be supported by the evidence of other Pauline letters, such as Ephesians, where there are some similar ideas, including the idea of 'praying' and 'standing' in face of the temptations and pressures of the world (Ephesians 6.13, 18).

Suffering

We saw how important a theme suffering is for Paul in 1 Thessalonians, and in 3.3–4 he urges them not to be unsettled by the trials they are facing: 'You know quite well that we were destined for them. In fact, when we were with you, we kept telling you that we would be persecuted. And it turned out that way.' Paul's teaching on this subject could have arisen quite simply from his own painful experience, not from any teaching of Jesus. On the other hand, his comment about Christians 'being destined' for trials may suggest that he had some solid theological basis for his comments. We wondered if Paul was echoing Mark 13.10–13 in 1 Thessalonians 2.14–16, and when looking at Galatians we wondered if Paul was influenced by Jesus' teaching on taking up the cross. There is plenty of other teaching of Jesus in the gospels about suffering, including the beatitude 'Blessed are those who are persecuted for righteousness' sake, for theirs is the kingdom of heaven' (Matthew 5.10; cf. Matthew 5.11; Luke 6.22). It is entirely possible that this teaching was passed on by Paul to the Thessalonians.

The kingdom and ethics

1 Thessalonians is like Galatians in that there is very little reference to the kingdom of God. But there is one reference in 2.12, where Paul speaks of urging the Thessalonians 'to live lives worthy of God, who calls you into his kingdom and glory'. It is interesting that he can refer to the 'kingdom' of God when writing to his Greek-speaking readers, and we may legitimately conclude that he had taught them about it. It is also interesting that here, as in Galatians and in 1 Corinthians, the kingdom is mentioned as something making high ethical demands.

Paul takes up the ethical theme in chapter 4, where he says, 'you know what instructions we gave you through the Lord Jesus', and then proceeds to warn against sexual immorality and to advocate holiness and purity (4.2, 3–8). The phrase 'through the Lord Jesus Christ' may be a clue that he is here specifically recalling the teaching of Jesus, who was outspoken in his call for sexual purity and whose teaching on marriage is certainly quoted by Paul in 1 Corinthians 7.10–11.

In 1 Thessalonians 4.3–4 Paul urges the Thessalonians to keep themselves from immorality, and says (literally) that 'each of you should know how to get his own vessel in holiness and honour, not in the passion of desire'. Scholars have puzzled over the word 'vessel'. It seems quite probable that Paul is referring to people's bodies, and it could be that he uses the word 'vessel' because he is recalling the teaching of Jesus about holiness and purity: Jesus spoke about the importance of inner purity, and used the example of cups and dishes that are clean outside and dirty inside (e.g. Luke 11.37–41; cf. Mark 7.18–23). This is a rather speculative possibility, though we shall later see more solid proof of Paul's knowledge of Jesus' teaching about purity.

From the commands about sexual purity Paul moves on to the subject of brotherly love, commenting that he does not need to write to them about this, 'for you yourselves have been taught by God to love one another' (4.9). The words 'love one another' are exactly those used in John's gospel of Jesus' new commandment, which we discussed in connection with 'the law of Christ' in Galatians 6.2. Paul refers to the Thessalonians knowing this love principle very well already, which would fit in with the conclusion that it was a tradition of Jesus that had been passed on. However, what Paul actually says is that they had been 'taught by God to love one another', which is most likely a reference to the Holy Spirit producing the fruit of love (cf. Galatians 5.22; Isaiah 54.13; Jeremiah 31.33–4). Paul will come back to the same theme in 5.13, where he urges the Thessalonians to 'be at peace among yourselves'; according to Mark 9.50 Jesus encouraged his followers to 'be at peace with one another', and we may suspect that Paul is echoing Jesus in these injunctions.

Conclusion

We have investigated Paul's use of stories and sayings of Jesus in Galatians and now in 1 Thessalonians. We have seen plenty of evidence suggesting such use in both letters. Interestingly, some of the evidence overlaps; for example, both Galatians and 1 Thessalonians bring out the 'love one another' theme. But most of the traditions of Jesus drawn on in 1 Thessalonians are different from those used in Galatians. This is simple to explain. Paul's agenda in Galatians is determined by the Judaizing crisis and the questioning of his apostleship; we therefore find a very strong emphasis on the cross of Jesus and a keen interest in the question of apostles and apostleship, but very little interest in the second coming of the Lord. In 1 Thessalonians on the other hand, the questions are to do with the second coming and the experience of persecution, and we find Jesus' eschatological teaching surfacing again and again. On the other hand, anti-Pauline Jewish Christianity does not seem to be a major issue with the Thessalonians, and the cross and the resurrection are mentioned quite briefly (1.10, 2.15, 4.14, 5.10); questions to do with apostleship are not dwelt on, though in 2.6 he mentions apostles and their right to support (a theme we will return to when looking at 1 Corinthians).

The theological detective looking at this evidence will not be too mystified: what is clear is that in these two letters Paul is not giving a comprehensive recap of his earlier teaching; rather he is responding to burning local issues. So we would be totally wrong to think that Paul did not say much to the Galatians about the second coming because it is not prominent in Galatians, just as we would be totally wrong to think that the cross and resurrection of Jesus were not important in Paul's teaching to the Thessalonians because it does not feature much in his letter to them. We would also be very unwise to conclude that Paul does not know stories and sayings of Jesus to which he does not allude in his letters; after all, we would have no idea from Galatians that Paul knew much of Jesus' eschatological teaching, but 1 Thessalonians puts us right on this. It is significant that in both letters stories and sayings of Jesus seem to lie behind Paul's teaching. It begins to look as though the traditions of Jesus were important in almost every connection.

11   A look at 2 Thessalonians

Paul's second letter to the Thessalonians is in many ways very similar to 1 Thessalonians:

- it is from Paul, Silas and Timothy again (1.1);
- it refers to the Thessalonians suffering at the hands of their enemies (1.1–10);
- it focuses strongly on the second coming (1.7–10, 2.1–12);
- it urges the Thessalonians to work hard and not to be busybodies (3.6–12).

The natural assumption, and indeed the traditional view, is that the letter was written quite soon after 1 Thessalonians, in a similar historical context. 1 Thessalonians had been delivered, and then further news came to Paul, and he picks up his pen again. It is quite literally part 2 of the correspondence.

On this view, what has Paul heard? First, that the Thessalonians are still having a hard time; maybe persecution has even intensified, since Paul does not mince his words about the judgement that he says will come on 'those who trouble you' (1.6). In 1 Thessalonians he spoke about how the Lord's return would bring comfort and resurrection to believers, but now he speaks of how the Lord will come in 'blazing fire' and 'will punish those who do not know God and do not obey the gospel of our Lord Jesus. They will be punished with everlasting destruction and shut out from the presence of the Lord and from the majesty of his power on the day he comes to be glorified with his holy ones and to be marvelled at among all those who have believed' (1.7–10).

Second, he has heard that the Thessalonians have been unsettled and alarmed by the idea that 'the day of the Lord has already come' (2.1). Paul seems unsure where this idea has come from, but mentions 'some prophecy, report or letter supposed to have come from us' (2.2). Whatever the origin of the idea, Paul replies by reminding them of his earlier teaching about 'that day': he had taught them that the day would be preceded by the 'rebellion' and the revealing of 'the

111

man of lawlessness', who 'opposes and exalts himself over everything that is called God ... and even sets himself up in God's temple, proclaiming himself to be God' (2.3–4). Paul goes on to say that this has not yet happened, and that this mysterious man of lawlessness is at present being held back by 'the one who now holds it back'. But the time will come when this man of lawlessness will be revealed and will deceive people by his power, before being destroyed together with his followers by Jesus at his coming (2.5–12).

Paul's teaching here is as mysterious as any in his letters, and scholars have had a field day coming up with ideas about what sort of figure this 'man of lawlessness' is: is he a human figure, perhaps a Roman emperor? Is he a spiritual Antichrist figure of some sort, or even the devil himself? And who is 'the one who is now holding him back'? Is this one a human figure, maybe the Roman emperor again upholding law and order? Or, to take a quite different approach, is he Paul, in his special capacity as apostle to the Gentiles whose work must be completed before the Lord's return? Or is he an angelic or demonic figure? Or is 'he' a symbolic figure – the rule of law and order, which holds back evil, or the preaching of the Christian good news? There are many possibilities. Whatever the answer, the general force of Paul's answer is clear enough; he is telling the Thessalonians to cool off, since the Lord's return has not yet begun.

The third thing that Paul has heard is that some people in the church are being idle and so causing trouble (3.8). We suggested, when looking at 1 Thessalonians, that they may have been abusing the generosity of the Christian fellowship. Whether they were also appealing to the nearness of the Lord's return as an excuse for their idleness is impossible to tell. In any case, Paul is stronger in 2 Thessalonians than he was in the first letter in commanding the offenders to work, in warning that they should not be fed if they will not work (3.10), and in suggesting that those who persist in disobedience may need to be excluded temporarily from the church community (3.14).

Doubts about 2 Thessalonians

Some scholars have felt that the teaching of 2 Thessalonians is significantly different from 1 Thessalonians, and so cannot be from

Paul, despite what it claims. It is argued, among other things, that the tone is harsher than 1 Thessalonians, with a strong emphasis on divine judgement; it is argued that the teaching about things happening before the Lord's return (e.g. the appearance of the man of lawlessness) is at odds with the emphasis on suddenness in 1 Thessalonians. The letter is, therefore, seen as pseudonymous, i.e. as falsely named: some Christian teacher produced this letter, modelling it on 1 Thessalonians (hence the similarities between the two letters), but setting out his own ideas, and ascribing the finished product to 'Paul, Silas and Timothy'. Scholars have argued that this was quite commonly done, and that it was not necessarily sinister or deliberately deceptive, but a recognized way of honouring a great teacher and his authority, as one tried to apply their teaching to new situations.

A quite different suggestion made by other scholars is that 2 Thessalonians preceded 1 Thessalonians. It is claimed that 2 Thessalonians refers to the Thessalonian Christians' suffering at that moment (1.4–7), which would fit the situation soon after Paul's departure, whereas in 1 Thessalonians the sufferings seem less acute and more in the past (1.6, etc.). And in 2 Thessalonians Paul has to correct the Thessalonians' imminent expectation of the Lord's return (2.1–3), whereas in 1 Thessalonians that misunderstanding has been put right and 'we do not need to write to you' about the question of the time (5.1).

However, neither of these views is very persuasive. A number of points are worth making.

First, the evidence that pseudonymity was a well-accepted way of writing letters in Christian circles in New Testament times is not strong, as has been shown by the recent thesis of my Oxford colleague, Jeremy Duff. In 2 Thessalonians the author himself can conceive of a 'letter falsely supposed to have come from us', but he objects to any such letter and implies that his letter is genuine (2.2). He makes the same claim at the end of the letter, where he says, 'I, Paul, write this greeting in my own hand, which is the distinguishing mark in all my letters. This is how I write' (3.17). One might see in this verse the author revealing his bad conscience about writing pseudonymously; in that case it is clear that this is not a respectable way of writing. Indeed the author seems to be going out of his way to deceive us. So the letter is a disreputable forgery – or it is genuinely what it claims to be.

Second, the differences in tone between the letters make very good sense in the traditionally assumed historical context. Paul's tone in 1 Thessalonians is enormously positive, because of his relief at the good news he has received of a church he loved and that is basically in good order (though he could say harsh things about those hindering the Christian gospel: 2.14–16). His tone in 2 Thessalonians is understandably less happy: he has not been so worried this time and thus he is not so relieved; also the problems seem to have worsened in some ways, despite his exhortations in 1 Thessalonians.

Third, the fact that Paul does not focus on the things happening before the end in 1 Thessalonians is because that was not the issue. The issue was: what has happened to those who have died before the Lord's return? To answer that question, Paul describes the Lord's return. He does not need to say what will happen before the Lord's return; indeed he says that he thinks they know all about times and dates, and he simply reminds them of the suddenness of the Lord's return and of the importance of keeping awake and sober for it (5.1–10). In 2 Thessalonians, however, Paul has to address the question of times and dates directly, because he hears that some of them are saying that the day of the Lord has arrived. In this context Paul has to calm them down, not to wake them up.

Fourth, it actually makes very good sense to see 1 Thessalonians as leading to 2 Thessalonians. In 1 Thessalonians the main thing about the 'times and the dates' that Paul does emphasize strongly is that they should keep awake, because the day of the Lord will come unexpectedly (5.1–3). 2 Thessalonians may be seen in part as dealing with a response to Paul's injunction – some of the Thessalonians are getting too wakeful and excited! (The opposite order is not so natural: if the Thessalonians were too excited about the imminence of the Lord's return, so that Paul had to calm them down in 2 Thessalonians, would he then in a follow-up letter, i.e. 1 Thessalonians on this theory, have emphasized the suddenness of the Lord's coming and the need to keep awake?)

Something in 1 Thessalonians that might particularly have excited the Thessalonians is the reference in 2.16 to the 'wrath having come' on the Jews at last. To us that phrase may sound obscure, but the Thessalonians will very likely have understood the puzzling reference. We have suggested that Paul was referring to the recent disasters to strike the Jews – in Rome and Jerusalem – and that these were seen as the divine 'wrath' that Jesus had promised would come on the Jewish nation, before the coming of the Son of Man. If the Thessalonians understood it that way, then it is not altogether surprising if some of them deduced that the end, looked forward to by Jesus, was breaking in. We can imagine that it was exactly the sort of idea which would have excited prophets (then as now), and that they in turn may have been stirring up the Thessalonians with dramatic prophecies about the Lord's imminent return. These would have been especially appealing in their situation of suffering and persecution, which may well have taken a turn for the worse since the writing of 1 Thessalonians (hence the strong statements about divine judgement in 2 Thessalonians 1.6–10).

Some such context would make sense of Paul's comment about the Thessalonians being 'unsettled or alarmed by some prophecy, report or letter supposed to have come from us, saying that the day of the Lord has already come' (2.2). Paul sounds as though he does not know exactly where the idea has come from, but it is not impossible that his own first letter was a factor.

Paul and Jesus in 2 Thessalonians

The future

We saw how Paul seems to use the teaching of Jesus extensively to answer the Thessalonians' anxieties in 1 Thessalonians. Does he do the same in 2 Thessalonians? If so, this may help our reflections on the authenticity of 2 Thessalonians.

The most interesting evidence in this regard is Paul's teaching about the 'man of lawlessness' in chapter 2. Paul asks the Thessalonians: 'Don't you remember that when I was with you I used to tell you these things?' (v. 5). What precisely were these things that Paul told them about?

Paul introduces the discussion with the phrase 'concerning the coming of our Lord Jesus Christ and our being gathered to him'

(2.1). The word for 'coming' here is *parousia*, a word used in secular Greek for the coming of a political or other dignatory to a place. The word for 'being gathered' is the noun form of the word used in Mark 13, where Jesus refers to the coming Son of Man sending out his angels and 'gathering' his elect from the four winds (13.26; see also Matthew 24.31). The two phrases together remind us inevitably of the eschatological discourse of Jesus; Matthew's version of the discourse actually has Jesus use the word *parousia* (24.27, 37).

Paul goes on in 2 Thessalonians 2 to describe what will happen before the Lord's coming, focusing on the 'rebellion' and on the revelation of 'the man of lawlessness [...] the son of destruction': 'He opposes and exalts himself over everything that is called God or is worshipped, and even sets himself up in God's temple, proclaiming himself to be God' (2.3–4). Although Paul's meaning is vigorously debated by scholars, the background to his ideas is probably the catastrophe that came on the Jews in 167 BC at the hands of Antiochus, which we described in the previous chapter. As the man who tried to abolish the Jewish religion, Antiochus was the epitome of 'lawlessness'; he had a pagan altar set up in the Jerusalem temple, and he called himself 'Epiphanes', i.e. the 'manifestation', thus claiming divine status for himself. Paul tells the Thessalonians that an Antiochus-like figure must come before the Lord's parousia.

The events of 167 BC were never far from the minds of first-century Jews. They remembered them – and in particular the victory of the Maccabees and the rededication of the temple in 164 BC – every year in the Feast of Hanukkah (or Dedication), and they were reminded of the threat posed by a pagan superpower by the presence of the Romans in Jerusalem itself. In AD 39 it looked as though Antiochus's desecration was going to be repeated – disastrously. As we mentioned earlier, the megalomaniac Roman emperor, Gaius Caligula, who encouraged people to see him as divine, ordered his statue to be erected in the Jerusalem temple; there were tumultuous protests, which did not look like changing Caligula's mind. In fact he was assassinated before his order was carried out.

If the events of 167 BC, nearly repeated in AD 39, are the likely background to Paul's teaching about the man of lawlessness in 2 Thessalonians 2, we may still ask: where did he get the idea that something of this sort would precede the Lord's return? Was it his own original idea?

The interesting and significant thing is that Jesus, according to the gospels, predicted exactly such a disaster for the Jerusalem temple. Matthew and Mark describe Jesus as speaking of a terrible day coming, when 'the abomination of desolation' or 'the desolating sacrilege' would be set up in the Jerusalem temple, and when it would be wise for everyone in Jerusalem to flee to the mountains, which is what the Maccabees did in 167 BC (1 Maccabees 2:28, Mark 13.14, Matthew 24.15). The phrase 'abomination of desolation' is taken directly from the Old Testament book of Daniel and from the apocryphal First Book of Maccabees, both of which refer unambiguously to the pagan altar (and perhaps statue) which Antiochus set up in the temple (Daniel 9.27, 11.31; 1 Maccabees 1.54).

It turns out that both Jesus in his teaching about the future and Paul in 2 Thessalonians speak of a new Antiochus-like horror preceding the coming of the Son of Man. They both also speak about this horror being accompanied by deceptive 'signs and wonders' (Matthew 24.24; Mark 13.22; 2 Thessalonians 2.9–11).

The parallels are very striking, and indeed, there is a case for seeing 2 Thessalonians 2 almost as a brief précis of the teaching of Jesus in Matthew 24 and Mark 13 (see Table 11.1).

The parallels can hardly be accidental. Other evidence may be relevant too. For example, Paul speaks of 'the man of *lawlessness*, the son of *destruction*', which could be said to correspond to 'the *abomination* (something flagrantly contrary to the law) *of desolation*'

Table 11.1   *Parallels between the teaching of Jesus and Paul*

Matthew 24, Mark 13	2 Thessalonians 2
Opening warnings not to be deceived or disturbed	Warnings against being disturbed, 'let no one deceive you'
Abomination in the temple	Man of lawlessness in temple
Misleading signs and wonders	Misleading signs and wonders
The coming of the Son of Man and gathering of the elect	The coming of the Lord (and gathering of the elect)

(something bringing devastation). Matthew's gospel, in the verses immediately before the passage about the abomination, speaks of 'the multiplication of lawlessness' (24.12); it is possible that in his version of Jesus' teaching the abomination is seen as illustrating that lawlessness. In any case we see that there are unmistakable thematic links between the teaching of Jesus in the gospels and the teaching of 2 Thessalonians 2.

Paul says that he is reminding the Thessalonians of what he has taught them: 'don't you remember that when I was with you I used to tell you these things?' (2.5). In view of this and in view of what we have seen, it seems entirely likely that he has passed on to them Jesus' teaching about the future. This is all the more likely given the evidence we have noted in 1 Thessalonians for Paul's familiarity with Jesus' teaching about his future return. On the basis of 1 Thessalonians we might almost have expected Paul to know what 2 Thessalonians shows him to have known!

The argument might appear to be complicated by the fact that we have noted Paul having things in common sometimes with Mark, sometimes with Matthew, sometimes with Luke. But, as we saw before, this is only a problem given an improbably rigid view of gospel relationships, which sees Matthew and Luke as wholly dependent on Mark in passages such as Jesus' eschatological discourse. In fact there is good reason for believing that in the eschatological discourse Matthew and Luke record at least some sayings of Jesus that do not come from Mark (e.g. Matthew 24.10–12; Luke 21.20–4, 34–6). Paul's evidence would tend to support this. So would common sense: a church that was very taken up with the hope of Jesus' imminent return is likely to have had more sayings and versions of sayings of Jesus than simply those preserved in Mark's gospel. There is every likelihood that Matthew, Luke and Paul will have known such material.

Our suggested conclusion, therefore, is that Paul had told the Thessalonians about the Lord's return and about how it would be preceded by judgement on the Jews, disaster in Jerusalem, and distress on earth. When he wrote to them in 1 Thessalonians about 'the wrath' coming on the Jews, the Thessalonians rightly understood this to mean the beginning of the promised judgement. Perhaps they had heard specifically of the disgraceful action of the Roman soldier in the temple, and saw that as something to do with the promised 'abomination'; perhaps there were famines and other distressing events such as they expected in the last days. They thus got overexcited, deducing that it was already the day of the Lord. So Paul has to remind them that, although lawlessness was indeed already manifesting itself, there was much more to come before the day of the Lord; the temple would be defiled and made desolate through the actions of the 'man of lawlessness'. That sort of catastrophe did not occur until the Jewish war of AD 66–70 and the subsequent destruction of the temple by the Romans.

Whether Jesus' teaching throws any light on Paul's comment about the 'one who now holds back' the man of lawlessness is unclear. In both Matthew and Mark Jesus speaks about the necessity that the gospel be preached to the nations before the coming of the Son of Man (Matthew 24.14; Mark 13.10; Luke does not have this saying, but in 21.24 Jesus speaks of the 'times of the Gentiles'), and this could support the view that it is the preaching of the gospel that is holding off the coming of the lawless one. We noticed before that Paul's reference in Romans 11.25 to the 'full number of the Gentiles coming in' could be linked to the words of Luke 21.24 about 'the times of the Gentiles being fulfilled'. Certainly there is a sense in Paul's letters that his mission to the Gentiles has eschatological significance: he is fulfilling the Old Testament promises about the Gentiles coming into God's people, and he wants to complete the task of spreading the good news of Christ to the Gentiles, so that God's purpose of redemption for the whole world, Jew and Gentile, may be fulfilled (see especially Romans 11.11–32, 15.9–29).

Other links to Jesus

A few other things in 2 Thessalonians may be linked with the teaching of Jesus:

- 1.3 has a reference to loving one another.
- 1.5 speaks about the Thessalonians being counted worthy 'of the kingdom of God, because of their sufferings'. The use of kingdom language is interesting and the saying reminds us of the beatitude that describes the kingdom of heaven as belong-

ing to those who are persecuted for righteousness' sake (Matthew 5.10).

- 1.5–9 speak of blazing fire and punishment for those who do not obey the gospel, and who will be purged from the presence of God. Several of Jesus' parables about the future have solemn warnings of exclusion from God's presence and of the fire of God's judgement (e.g. Matthew 25.10–13, 13.30, 42).

These last links prove little, if anything, but the earlier observations about 2 Thessalonians 2 are very significant: they tend to confirm the view that 2 Thessalonians is genuinely from Paul, not a fake, forgery or pseudonymous letter, and, if that is correct, they confirm that Paul knew and passed on to the Thessalonians the teachings of Jesus about the future contained in his eschatological discourse.

12 Travelling on to Ephesus

What happened next according to Acts?

We have spent a long time with Paul in Corinth in the last few chapters – appropriately, since Paul spent a long time there, a year and a half according to Acts 18.11, and perhaps longer (v. 18). But then, according to Acts, he sailed across the Aegean Sea to Ephesus with Priscilla and Aquila. He seems to have stayed there only briefly, since he was headed for Jerusalem and Antioch. Acts refers to him having his hair cut off 'because of a vow he had taken' (18.18). Jews made vows for various purposes, including the giving of thanks for past blessings; such vows typically would have included the shaving of the head and abstinence from alcohol, and would have ended with the offering of a sacrifice in Jerusalem. Acts very briefly describes Paul going to Jerusalem and greeting the church there (18.22). We get the impression that it was a quick visit, which would be understandable, given Paul's history. Then Paul went on to Antioch. How long he stayed there is not clear, but Acts soon has him back on the road, headed for Galatia and Phrygia again, visiting the churches that he and Barnabas had founded.

Acts mentions at this point a man who will be an important player in the story, Apollos (18.24–8). Apollos came from Alexandria in Egypt. Alexandria was one of the Roman Empire's great cities, with a large population of perhaps a million people, including a large Jewish community. It was a centre of learning, boasting a huge and famous library and a research centre called the Museum. It was the place where the famous Greek translation of the Old Testament, the Septuagint, was produced in the three centuries before the time of Christ, and it was also the home city of Philo, a famous Jewish philosopher and writer of the first century AD, who sought to combine the best of Greek and Jewish learning.

Apollos is described in Acts as a 'learned' (*logios*) man, 'powerful in the Scriptures' (18.24). He had been taught 'the way of the Lord' and about Jesus, and was 'fervent [literally 'boiling'] in spirit'

121

(18.25). He came to Ephesus, where he preached about Jesus in the synagogue. According to Acts, Priscilla and Aquila heard him, but his understanding of the Christian way was deficient because he 'knew only the baptism of John' (18.25). Exactly what this means is debatable. Acts goes on in 19.1–6 to describe twelve 'disciples', who seem to have something in common with Apollos: they knew about John the Baptist and his baptism, but did not know about baptism in the name of Jesus and the associated gift of the Holy Spirit. Such half-taught Christians (if indeed these twelve are seen in Acts as Christians) may seem odd to us, but there is no reason in principle why people in places like Alexandria and Ephesus should not have heard about John the Baptist and even about Jesus, but not have caught up with the later developments in the Christian church. In any case Acts describes Priscilla and Aquila instructing Apollos, and Paul later instructing the deficient disciples, who were duly baptized in the name of Jesus and received the Holy Spirit.

Apollos, we are told by Acts, went on from Ephesus to Achaia, and in particular to Corinth, where he was 'a great help to those who by grace had believed', engaging in effective debate with the Jews of Corinth (18.27–8).

Paul meanwhile had come to Ephesus, and begun a lengthy period of ministry there. Acts describes him adhering to his now traditional pattern of ministry. He began in the synagogue, speaking boldly there over three months and 'arguing persuasively about the kingdom of God'. Then, as usual, things turned sour, and Paul moved to the 'lecture hall' of one Tyrannus, where he had daily discussions with people for two years, 'so that all the Jews and Greeks who lived in the province of Asia heard the word of the Lord' (19.9–10). 'Asia' here means the province, of which Ephesus was the main city.

Acts suggests that Paul's ministry in Asia was very powerful and effective, his words being accompanied by remarkable miracles (19.11–16). Such a ministry had a major impact on other religions. Acts refers to people abandoning their magic, for which the city was well known, and burning their books of spells. The figure of 50,000 drachmas is given for their value, which is impressive when we realize that a drachma was a labourer's daily wage. More serious still was the impact on the temple of Artemis, the great pride of

Ephesus. Artemis was the Greek goddess of hunting, but as worshipped in Ephesus she seems to be a cross between the Greek goddess and a local fertility goddess. Her temple there was huge, one of the seven wonders of the world and an important pilgrimage centre, and thus an important source of revenue to the city. Acts says that it was the craftsmen who made and sold silver shrines for people to buy as souvenirs or religious objects who were initially upset by Paul's ministry, because he was taking away their customers. The result was a major riot, some of Paul's companions being seized and brought into the famous city theatre. Eventually the furious crowd, which is described as chanting for two hours 'Great is Artemis of the Ephesians', was pacified by the city clerk. But this traumatic business led to Paul's departure from Ephesus en route for Macedonia (20.1). Acts tells us that he had already sent his colleagues Timothy and Erastus there, and that his plan was to visit Macedonia and Achaia, then to go to Jerusalem and then to Rome (19.21).

Such is the account of Acts. The story is clearly a very selective and brief account of a ministry lasting several years, but it makes perfect sense in the light of what we know of Ephesus from historical sources and archaeology. The references to magic practices, to the temple of Artemis and its 'image which fell from heaven' (probably a meteorite), to the theatre (the ruins of which still survive) and to various local officials (the city clerk, the Asiarchs and the proconsuls), all make good sense.

What happened next according to Paul?

But what of Paul's letters? Do they confirm the Acts account? 1 Corinthians is of most interest in this respect. It was evidently written from Asia, since Paul says in 16.19, 'The churches in the province of Asia send you greetings. Aquila and Priscilla greet you warmly in the Lord, and so does the church that meets at their house.' These greetings are interesting, confirming what Acts tells us about Aquila and Priscilla going to Ephesus and about the establishment of churches in Asia. The establishment of churches across Asia may also be confirmed indirectly by the letter to the Colossians, since it has been plausibly suggested that the church in

Colossae (a town up the Lycus Valley, inland from Ephesus) and the neighbouring churches of Laodicea and Hierapolis were all founded in this period, not all by Paul personally, but in the case of Colossae by Epaphras, one of Paul's colleagues (1.7, 4.13).

The opening of 1 Corinthians is also interesting, since the letter is written in the name of 'Paul [...] and our brother Sosthenes'. A Sosthenes is mentioned as 'the synagogue ruler' in Corinth in Acts 18.17, as we saw before, and the fact that Acts mentions his name there makes it quite likely that he became a Christian and then went with Paul to Ephesus. Acts suggests that Paul had various companions from Greece with him in Ephesus: Aquila and Priscilla and Gaius and Aristarchus are those it names (19.29).

1 Corinthians also confirms that Apollos had a powerful ministry in Corinth after Paul's founding visit, so much so that there seems to have been a division in the church between supporters of Apollos and supporters of Paul (1.12, chs. 3 and 4). It seems that the followers of Apollos liked his eloquence and wisdom, which they rated higher than Paul's (2.1, etc.)! We might be tempted to think this situation similar to what had happened in Galatia, with people coming in and undermining Paul's work; but Acts suggests that Apollos was encouraged and helped by Priscilla and Aquila, and in 1 Corinthians Paul speaks positively of his ministry (16.12), confirming that Apollos himself is in fellowship with, not opposition to, Paul.

Acts, as we noticed, refers not only to Apollos, but to twelve 'disciples' in Ephesus, who did not know about baptism in the name of Jesus or about the Holy Spirit. Paul met with them, taught them, baptized them in Jesus' name and laid his hands on them. The result is that they received the Holy Spirit, and began to 'speak in tongues' and to prophesy (19.1–7). Speaking in 'tongues' or 'languages' – *glossa* in Greek can mean either or both – is mentioned several times in Acts (2.4, 10.45–6 and 19.6; cf. 8.17); the Holy Spirit comes on people, and they then speak in a spiritual 'tongue' or language. Most famous is the Day of Pentecost, when the disciples in Jerusalem spoke in tongues and the multi-national crowd 'each heard them speaking in his own language' (2.6). In other cases in Acts there is no evidence that the 'tongue' was a known language. This portrayal of Paul being involved in a spiritual ministry that involved people speaking in tongues is confirmed by his letters, and in particular by 1 Corinthians (a letter written from Ephesus, precisely in the period described by Acts 19). We shall say more about that in the next chapter.

1 Corinthians does not refer definitely to the riot in Ephesus, and may well have been written before it took place. But Paul does refer to 'many adversaries' (16.9), and it is just possible that 'I fought wild beasts in Ephesus' (15.32) is a figurative allusion to the traumatic events that included the riot; on the other hand, it could refer to some other terrifying experience of Paul's known to the Corinthians. 1 Corinthians does confirm Paul's itinerary as portrayed by Acts: he has come to Ephesus from Galatia (16.1), and his plan is to go from Ephesus to Macedonia, Achaia and then to Jerusalem (16.3–5). 1 Corinthians confirms that Timothy has gone ahead of Paul (16.10).

2 Corinthians was written after Paul left Ephesus, and confirms that he moved on from Ephesus to Troas and Macedonia (2.12–13). Paul refers back in 2 Corinthians to 'hardships we suffered in the province of Asia. We were under great pressure, far beyond our ability to endure, so that we despaired even of life' (1.8). This could well be a reference to the riot in the theatre and to the events leading up to that, since that sequence of events must have been hugely threatening and frightening for Paul and his followers; and the riot seems to lead in Acts to Paul's departure from Ephesus. (Note also that Acts 19.29 refers to two companions of Paul caught up in the riot, Gaius and Aristarchus. We meet these names again in 1 Corinthians 1.14, Romans 16.23, Colossians 4.10, and Philemon 24. We cannot be sure, however, that they are the same individuals.) However, the awful suffering referred to in 2 Corinthians 1.8 might be some other crisis which Acts does not describe. In Romans 16.4 Paul speaks of Priscilla and Aquila risking their lives for him, which may have been in Ephesus. Some scholars have speculated that Paul may have been imprisoned in the city for a while (cf. 2 Corinthians 11.23).

1 Corinthians, 2 Corinthians and also Romans make it clear that a major project for Paul in this period was a collection of money for the church in Jerusalem (1 Corinthians 16.1–3; 2 Corinthians 8—9; Romans 16.23–9); Romans also confirms that Paul's intention was

to go on from Jerusalem to Rome, and indeed from Rome to Spain. Acts, interestingly, only has a passing reference to the collection (24.17), but it does make it clear that Paul was accompanied by representatives of various of the donor churches (including Ephesus: 21.29).

In conclusion, there are various points where Paul's letters directly and unambiguously confirm the Acts account of his ministry in and around Ephesus; there are various other points where Acts and the letters may converge, though we cannot prove this. There is nothing to make us doubt the trustworthiness of Acts' account of this part of Paul's ministry.

13 What is going on in 1 Corinthians?

Of all the churches that Paul founded we know most about the church in Corinth. Paul wrote a number of letters to the church there, two of which survive. The first of these is particularly informative, giving us all sorts of insight into what a Pauline church was like, and also into Paul's ministry.

What then was going on? What were the issues they faced, and how does Paul respond to them? We could answer these questions by working systematically through 1 Corinthians from the beginning; but I propose instead to start near the end of the letter and to look at Paul's discussion of the worship and spirituality of the Corinthian church, since this will give us clues that will illuminate other parts of the letter.

If this seems a topsy-turvy approach, maybe that is appropriate for what was a rather topsy-turvy church! But our starting point may also be justified from Paul's thanksgiving in 1.4–7, where he thanks God for the Corinthians and for the fact that 'you do not lack any spiritual gift as you eagerly wait for our Lord Jesus Christ to be revealed'. We notice from this that, like their Thessalonian neighbours, the Corinthians were looking forward to the return of the Lord; we observed before that 'Maranatha', an Aramaic cry for the Lord to come, was an important ingredient in their liturgy (16.22). But we also notice how Paul, as often, flags up key issues in his opening thanksgiving which he will come back to in the letter. One very important issue for the Corinthians was the issue of the Spirit.

A spiritual church

If we could have gone along to the Corinthian church with a video camera on a Sunday (which is when they appear to have met for worship:16.2), what would we have seen and heard? The answer is that we would have found a spiritually gifted church or, to use modern terminology, a 'charismatic' church, worshipping in an informal way with spiritual gifts very much in evidence. In particular we would have found lots of speaking in tongues and prophesying (14.26–32). The services seem to have been rather chaotic, with people speaking in tongues all over the place, no one explaining the meaning of what was being said and different people speaking at the same time.

Not surprisingly it seems that this was divisive and that, although some people spoke in tongues, and very enthusiastically, others did not. It seems likely that the tongues-speakers saw the non-tongues-speakers as unspiritual. For the tongues-speakers the gift of tongues was normative, given to them very likely in their baptism, and they probably saw it as a heavenly language – what else? (ch. 13.1, 'the tongues of angels'). They were excited to be living in the new age of the Spirit and to be experiencing the powers of the kingdom of God. The non-tongues-speakers probably disliked the chaos, objected to being regarded as spiritually inferior and quite possibly objected to the whole tongues-speaking business.

Paul's comment on the situation is masterly: he, like the more charismatic Corinthians, is excited by the Holy Spirit's work in the life of the Church, but he insists that all baptized Christians (not just those who speak in tongues) have the Spirit (12.12–13). 'Jesus is Lord' seems to have been the confession of faith that people would make when being baptized (Romans 10.9), and Paul says: 'No one can say, "Jesus is Lord", except by the Holy Spirit' (1 Corinthians 12.3).

He goes on to say that there are different gifts, not just tongues, all given by the same Holy Spirit, as the Spirit determines. Paul explains this through his famous image of the body with different parts (12.14–26). He makes the point that we need different parts in the body, and not just the more visible glamorous parts, and that the parts need to work together. The application to the Corinthian church is obvious enough, and Paul is quite clear that not everyone speaks in tongues or needs to. In the Greek, the question in 12.30 'Do all speak in tongues?' is a question expecting the answer no. It is significant that in his various lists of gifts in chapter 12 Paul consistently puts tongues at the bottom (vv. 10, 30), whereas many of the Corinthians would have put it very high in their estimation.

Paul goes on in his famous chapter 13 to make the point that love is more important by far than any spiritual gifts, wonderful though those gifts are, and also more lasting. The Corinthians may think that tongues are the language of the angels, but Paul says that tongues will pass away. The language of heaven will be love, rather than tongues, and it is this gift of love that Paul urges the divided Corinthians to cultivate. In Galatians, as we saw, Paul lists love as the first fruit of the Spirit (5.22), and he wants the Corinthians to develop a spirituality with that priority.

Paul completes his discussion of spiritual gifts with some practical advice, advocating the use of intelligible prophecy rather than tongues, because the former 'builds up' the Church. Paul believes tongues to be a good gift of God, and agrees that it would be nice if everyone had them (14.5, but they don't – see chapter 12); he uses the gift himself – enthusiastically (14.18). But in public he himself would much rather speak in a way that could be understood, and he would have the Corinthians do the same. So Paul's practical instructions for sorting out the chaos are:

- only two or three tongues should be used in a service;
- tongues should only be used at all in public worship if interpreted by someone;
- people should not talk over one another, but give way to each other. It is a mark of truly spiritual prophets that they 'submit' to other prophets, rather than insist on doing their own thing. 'God is not a God of disorder but of peace' (14.27–33).

Some people have speculated that the Corinthians' charismatic spirituality, including speaking in tongues, was due to the influence of pagan religions of the time. But, although it is not possible to rule out all such influence, it seems entirely probable that speaking in tongues was part of the Christianity that Paul brought with him to Corinth. There is evidence of a similar spirituality in Thessalonica (1 Thessalonians 5.17), and Acts suggests that it was a feature of early Christianity from the beginning. So the Corinthians' charismatic spirituality was not a pagan aberration, but something they received from Paul and others. Whether their particular excesses owed anything to pagan influences is hard to say; their whackier ideas and practices could have arisen simply from a misunderstanding of Paul's teaching.

Women and men in Corinth

Our video camera would have noticed that women were taking a prominent part in the church's worship, not confining themselves to a submissive back-seat role in the manner of the Jewish synagogue. Some women were praying and prophesying publicly (11.3–16), and were causing controversy by doing so with their heads uncovered. This was evidently breaking with convention and was provocative. If they were married women, it may have looked as though they were casting aside their marriage veil and conventional morality. In any case they were acting like the men of the congregation, in a way that offended propriety in the eyes of some and certainly upset members of the congregation, probably including some of their husbands.

It seems that this problem too may have arisen partly out of Paul's teaching to the Corinthians. Paul had very likely taught them, as he had the Galatians, that 'there is neither Jew nor Greek, slave nor free, male nor female, for you are all one in Christ Jesus' (Galatians 3.28). The language here may well have been used in connection with baptism. Certainly for Paul there was oneness in baptism, and oneness among believers in the Spirit. It is understandable that this egalitarian teaching would have been very liberating for women converts to Christianity. Acts refers to various 'leading' women responding to Paul's evangelistic ministry 16.14, 17.3; in Corinth the women were taking part in the spiritual ministry of the church. That seemed to be fine, at least in Paul's eyes. But some of the spiritual women were taking their liberation and equality to mean that they could dress like the men in worship 'with heads uncovered', thus causing offence (cf. 2 Corinthians 3.18).

If this situation was partly of Paul's making, what was his response to it? As with the issue of speaking in tongues, Paul does not retract what he said; but in this case he makes it very clear that 'there is no male and female' does not mean that gender differences have all been superseded in the Christian life. In a complicated argument Paul refers the Corinthians back to the creation story of Adam and Eve, where Adam and Eve are created differently and where indeed Adam has priority. Paul makes it clear that this does not mean that woman is inferior (11.11–12), but it does mean that the Corinthians' unisex idea of life in Christ is wrong. God's creation (including sexual differences) is good, and being in the Spirit does not mean leaving the order of creation behind. It is interesting, and quite likely significant, that in 1 Corinthians 12.13 Paul says something similar to what he said in Galatians, but without reference to men and women: 'We were all baptized by one Spirit into one body – whether Jews or Greeks, slave or free'. His failure to include 'whether male or female' is not because he does not believe it – he does – but may well be because he knows that the Corinthians have unfortunately misunderstood that phrase.

In addition to the question of dress, there seems to have been some other issue relating to women in worship, which surfaces in 1 Corinthians 14.33–5. Paul has been discussing spiritual gifts and particularly tongues and prophecy, and he suddenly says that 'As in all the congregations of the saints, women should remain silent in the churches' (v. 34). This is a rather mysterious comment, given that back in chapter 11 Paul approves of women praying and prophesying. It seems likely that he is here referring to some particular disruptive activity that has been going on and adding to the chaos – perhaps wives (as the word 'women' may be translated) were claiming to be prophets and questioning or contradicting what their husbands were saying.

Relationships between the sexes are an important issue elsewhere in 1 Corinthians. There was a notorious case of immorality, of which the Corinthians seemed proud rather than ashamed (5.1). There were Corinthian men who were having sex with prostitutes and apparently justifying their actions by saying that 'everything is permissible for me' (6.12–20). On the other hand, there were some who were advocating total celibacy for Christians: a man should not 'touch' a woman (sexually), they argued; so the unmarried should stay unmarried, and the married should end their relationship and separate, especially when one of the married partners was still unconverted (ch. 7).

Once again it is possible to see this confusion as relating to Paul's earlier teaching. The idea that 'everything is permissible for me', which the Corinthians were also quoting in relation to the question as to whether Christians could eat food offered to idols (10.23), may reflect Graeco-Roman ideas about human freedom, but may also

131

have a rather direct connection with Paul's teaching about freedom from the law. We have seen how important that emphasis was for Paul when ministering in Galatia, and we can be sure that it was important to him in his ongoing ministry. Paul's teaching about Christian freedom primarily related to things like circumcision and the Jewish laws about clean and unclean food, but the Corinthians seem to have taken the idea of freedom to extremes, arguing that eating food offered to idols was acceptable (or 'clean', to use Paul's word) for Christians, as were other physical activities, including sexual intercourse with prostitutes. One suggestion is that the context for this teaching was drunken feasts in which sex with prostitutes was a regular part of the menu; were young Christian men claiming that such debauchery did no harm and was 'permissible'? Maybe this same 'liberated' attitude led the Corinthians to approve rather than to deplore the man who was living with his father's wife, though as Paul observes, this would have widely been seen as shocking immorality even in pagan circles (5.1).

It is unlikely that the Corinthians simply reached their conclusions on the basis of Paul's teaching: it seems likely that they were also influenced by the widespread Greek idea that the body is transient and relatively unimportant. The great philosopher Plato spoke of the 'body' (*soma* in Greek) as a 'tomb' (*sema*); it was seen as a shell that would eventually be discarded. It is easy to see how the Corinthians may have argued that Christians are 'spiritual' beings, and that it does not matter what we do with our bodies.

As for those in Corinth who were taking the opposite line and advocating sexual abstinence, one interesting suggestion is that this may have come in part at least from the spiritual women, who were taking a unisex approach to worship (ch. 11). If, after all, there is no male and female in Christ, as Paul had taught, then sexual intercourse between male and female must logically cease as well. In any case, if we are now spiritual beings, living in the Spirit and not in 'the flesh', as Paul had taught, then we are surely above earthly things such as sex! At the very least, they must have reasoned, the Christian should not defile himself or herself with a pagan partner.

This anti-sex line may seem surprising to us, but it is not so difficult to understand given the Christians' eager looking forward to the Lord's imminent return, the corruption of the world they lived in, the famines that we know to have hit the Roman world at about this time, which will have made family life difficult, their excited joy about being 'in the Spirit', and the celibacy of at least some of their models of Christian living, such as Paul himself. It is not difficult to imagine believers at that time trying to figure out what the Christian approach to spirituality and sex should be and coming up with the answer Paul reports in 1 Corinthians 7. The idea that it was some of the Corinthian women who were particularly advocating this line is suggested by the way Paul addresses them first in verse 10 and verses 39–40, and fits in with what we have seen about the liberated spiritual women, for whom spiritual ministry may well have seemed an obviously higher calling than marriage, child-bearing and domestic duties (cf. 1 Timothy 2.15, 4.3).

Paul replies to these various ideas of the Corinthians with a whole battery of arguments. Thus, he speaks categorically about how the wicked will not inherit the kingdom of God, listing 'the sexually immoral, idolaters, adulterers, male prostitutes, homosexual offenders,' etc. (6.9); he tells the Corinthians that they were once like that, but they have now been washed, sanctified and justified 'in the name of the Lord Jesus Christ and by the Spirit of our God' (6.11). The implication of this is that sexual immorality has no place in the Christian life.

Paul goes on to accept that in one sense 'everything is permissible', but he then quickly clarifies that this does not mean that everything is good (6.12; cf. also 10.23). In response to their view of the body as something spiritually unimportant, Paul asserts exactly the opposite, namely that the body belongs to the Lord, that the body will be raised from the dead (not just discarded), that the body is the temple of the Holy Spirit, and that the body should be used to glorify God (6.13–20). The Corinthian offenders saw sex as just a physical function like eating or drinking, and so sex with a prostitute was harmless. Paul saw sexual intercourse as much more than a casual physical encounter; he saw it as bringing about a significant union between the partners (a 'one-flesh' union, to use the language of Genesis 2.24, where Adam and Eve are made of the same stuff and belong together). So immorality is serious, and for a Christian who is united with Christ to have sex with a prostitute is unthinkable (6.13–18).

Paul has more time for the advocates of celibacy. He believes that celibacy is a high calling and that it does have value in the 'present crisis' (7.26, possibly a reference to a situation of famine) and in the short time remaining until the Lord returns, freeing people for ministry. But he believes that only some have this gift (7.7), and that others should marry and have sexual relations. Sex is not an unclean or unspiritual thing. Even in the case of a Christian whose spouse has not yet been converted, Paul does not believe that their having sex defiles the Christian partner (7.14). The Corinthians feared that the non-Christian partner would make the relationship (and the Christian partner and their children) 'unclean'. Paul argues that on the contrary the Christian partner 'sanctifies' the relationship and family – not in the sense that the non-Christian partner is saved through the relationship (though their salvation is something to be fervently hoped for: 7.16), but in the sense that the relationship is clean in the eyes of God and so not to be abandoned by the Christian partner.

Food matters

When the Corinthians met for worship, as we have seen, there were divisions over spiritual gifts and over the role of women in the Church. But they did not just meet to worship together and to minister to each other; they also ate a meal together. Unfortunately this too was a cause of unhappiness and division, so much so that Paul can comment that, judging by the reports he has heard, 'your meetings do more harm than good' (11.17). In theory their shared meal was the Lord's Supper. Paul suggests that what is going on can hardly be called the Lord's Supper (11.20).

What would our video have recorded in this connection? It seems that the church community was gathering together for a meal, presumably in the house of a wealthy member, and that the wealthy were feasting themselves, even getting drunk, while the poor members were actually going hungry. One possibility is that the rich were at what we might call the top tables and that they were getting the best food with the host. The poor, on the other hand, some of them slaves who will not have been free to come early to the feast, were out in the courtyard and were being excluded in more senses than one. Alternatively, it may have been the sort of dinner party at which guests brought their own food, and the rich were not sharing with the poor. Paul is shocked by this, and says that they are missing the point of the Lord's Supper with its focus on the Lord's death, that they should stop their disgraceful behaviour forthwith, and that they should care for each member of the body (11.17–34).

Food was also an issue in other contexts, particularly the question of food offered to idols (chs. 8–10). The background to this issue is twofold: first, almost all meat in the public meat markets will have been sacrificed in a pagan ritual; second, pagan festivals (including festivals in honour of the 'divine' Roman emperor) were high points on the Corinthian social calendar, and meat was given out to people free at those festivals. The question arose: what is the Christian to do about such food? The normal Jewish line would have been total abstinence in both cases. But some of the Corinthian Christians applied the idea that 'all things are permissible' to this issue, and argued that it did Christians no harm to eat food offered to dead idols. This was dividing Christian from Christian, some 'weaker' brothers and sisters being seriously offended by the liberty of the 'stronger'.

Some people think that this problem, like the problems at the Lord's Supper, had an economic dimension: the wealthy Christians who were used to eating meat prior to their conversion had no qualms about continuing to do so; the poor Christians, on the other hand, who used to eat meat only at idolatrous festivals, felt uneasy about eating it now as Christians, as did some of the Christians from a pious Jewish background.

Whatever the truth of this, Paul's reply is fourfold. First, he agrees that the physical eating of food offered to idols does no harm; the food is part of God's good creation, and not changed by being offered to an idol (10.26). But, second, he knows that some people have a sensitive conscience with regard to this matter, and argues that they should not be forced to go against their conscience (8.7–13). Third, it is an overriding priority for Christians not to cause their brothers and sisters to stumble spiritually, and it is better to give up 'my' freedom than to hurt another (8.9—9.23). Fourth,

Christians must be careful not to participate in the worship of idols, since this is demonic, incompatible with belonging to Christ, and dangerous because it will bring the Lord's judgement (ch. 10).

Leadership issues

We have observed how divided the Corinthian church was over issues, but it was also divided over individual church leaders. This comes out at the very beginning of the letter, where Paul says that he has heard 'that there are quarrels among you. What I mean is this: One of you says, "I follow Paul"; another "I follow Apollos"; another "I follow Cephas"; still another, "I follow Christ"' (1 Corinthians 1.11–12).

Whether there were four recognizable parties in the Corinthian church, or whether it was just a case of people arguing and favouring one or other leader, is not clear. It is certainly not difficult to see how some would have looked to Paul as the father of the church, others to Apollos as a particularly gifted teacher who had worked among them, and others to Peter (Cephas in Aramaic) as an important authority, being the recognized leader of the whole Church (cf. Matthew 16.18; Acts 1.15, etc.; Galatians 2.8–9). It is not difficult to imagine some taking the high ground and saying that they followed Christ, and not any lesser leader. From what follows in 1 Corinthians it looks as though the principal division focused on Paul and Apollos; thus in chapters 3 and 4 Paul refers only to himself and Apollos.

It looks as if 'wisdom' was a particular issue in the dispute, since Paul focuses a lot in these chapters on questions of wisdom, eloquence and foolishness. Wisdom and eloquence were especially prized in the Graeco-Roman world, and Corinth will have had its share of sophist teachers, who competed with each other for disciples, trying to outdo each other in rhetorical skill. What seems likely is that some in the Corinthian church were comparing Apollos with Paul, and finding Apollos wiser and more eloquent. It is likely that some of the fans of Apollos were his converts, whom he baptized; maybe some of them provided hospitality for Apollos in their homes and supported his ministry. This last point may lie behind Paul's discussion of his own self-support in chapter 9.

In response to this situation Paul uses a variety of arguments. He points out the error of divisions in general (1.13), since there is one saviour Christ. He comments that he is glad that he did not personally baptize many people (1.14–16); this is not because Paul had a low view of baptism, but because few people could claim to be 'of Paul' on the grounds that he had baptized them.

But then he comes to his major point, which is that what God has done through Jesus is almost the exact antithesis of the human wisdom that the Corinthians have been favouring. Thus the heart of the Christian message is the cross, and surely that idea – of God saving the world through an execution outside Jerusalem – is stupid by all the standards of the world; it is folly to Greeks, a stumbling block to Jews. Then there is the evidence of the people who have come into the Church: they have not been the wise and the powerful for the most part, but the simple and the weak. God does not seem to be as keen on the wise and eloquent as are the Corinthians! As for his own preaching, Paul speaks of his own renunciation of worldly wisdom and rhetoric. Some scholars have argued that Paul does use rhetorical methods in his letters to get his points over, but he clearly wants to distance himself from the manipulative oratory that was fashionable in his day and from the Corinthians' adulation of clever human leaders. Pride in human individuals and human wisdom is utterly misplaced; the Christian good news is a divine wisdom, revealed by the Spirit, not dependent on clever human preachers or teachers (1.18—2.16).

Paul goes on to make it clear that he and Apollos should not therefore be put on pedestals as competing authorities, but recognized as servants of the one God in his field, and accountable to him. The Corinthians should give up their damaging boasting in human leaders and human wisdom and get excited instead about God the creator and about Jesus as the foundation of the Church (3.1—4.7). Instead of bragging that they belong to Paul, Apollos or Cephas, they should realize that Paul, Apollos, Cephas and everything else belong to them – through Christ and God (3.21–3).

Paul sees the Corinthians as arrogant – in their boasting about their favoured leader and also in their view of themselves. They seemed to think that they had arrived spiritually. Paul suggests that this claim is curious, given that he and the other apostles are suffering all sorts of hardship and persecution – evidently they have not arrived yet (4.8–13)!

Spiritual arrogance, perhaps arising in part from their powerful charismatic experiences, seems to have been an important ingredient affecting all sorts of aspects of Corinthian church life. It affected their relationships with each other, their relationship to Paul and other leaders, their morality and/or immorality, their worship, and their attitude to food offered to idols. Paul deplores such arrogance and all human boasting, insisting that the only appropriate boasting is in God and in Christ and him crucified (1.31, 3.21; cf. Galatians 6.14; Romans 3.27).

Resurrection at last

The final divisive issue that Paul addresses at length in 1 Corinthians is the question of the resurrection of the dead (chapter 15). Some in Corinth were denying that Christians who die are raised to life. We don't know exactly what they were saying:

- Were they denying all life after death, as some of the Greeks did?
- Did they believe in the immortality of the soul, as Greeks tended to, but not in the resurrection of the body? It seems likely that some of them did have a low view of the body, as we saw when considering the men who thought that immorality would not harm them (6.12–20).
- Did they think that they were experiencing the life to come already, through their experience of the Spirit, so there was no need for anything more? Did speaking in the tongues of angels show this? Does this lie behind the repudiation by some of them of all sexual intercourse? (It is interesting how in 1 and 2 Timothy there are references to people who say that the resurrection has happened already and to people who oppose marriage: 2 Timothy 2.18; 1 Timothy 4.3. Paul, if he is the author of these letters, affirms the goodness of creation, and also of childbearing (2.15).)
- Were they, like the Thessalonians, expecting the Lord to return very soon and thus not taking seriously the possibility that Christians might die and then rise again?

We have seen that different views (e.g. on sex) were represented among the Corinthians, and it seems quite likely that they had different views and different doubts about resurrection. Certainly Paul's reply can be seen to be addressing a variety of issues.

In response to their doubts, Paul says that,

1. Jesus rose from the dead: this is very well attested and at the heart of the Christian good news (15.1–11).
2. If that belief is abandoned, then the Christian faith as a whole is undermined (15.12–19).
3. In fact Christ has been raised, and he is the new life-bringing Adam. The Adam of Genesis brought death to the human race. Christ rose from the dead: he is the prototype of our resurrection, and he is one through whom God is overcoming evil and bringing the whole of creation back under his rule (15.20–8).
4. Neither the Corinthian practice of baptism for the dead, nor Paul's risking his life in the service of Christ in Ephesus, make sense if there is no resurrection (15.29–34). Unfortunately, we don't know either what the Corinthians' baptism for the dead involved (the video camera would be especially useful here!) or what Paul's 'fighting with the wild beasts in Ephesus' was.
5. On the question of the nature of the resurrection body: the Christian's dead body will be transformed as a seed is transformed into a plant; we will have a spiritual body like that of the risen Jesus (15.35–49).
6. What will happen on the last day is that the Christian dead will be raised with Christ, and death will be finally vanquished; Christ's victory will be complete (15.51–7).

Chaos in Corinth!

Paul heard about the goings-on in the Corinthian church from people who had come to him from Corinth (1.11, 11.17) and through a letter (7.1). Paul could justifiably have felt profoundly depressed that so much seemed to have gone wrong in the three years since he founded the church; Christians, presumably wealthy Christians, were even taking other Christians to court (6.1–11). Not for nothing does he speak in 2 Corinthians 11.28 of 'the pressure of my concern for all the churches'.

But perhaps it is not surprising that the Corinthians were mixed up. Given the following ingredients –

- the spiritual excitement and joy that the new Corinthian Christians experienced through the gospel and the Holy Spirit, which led some to think that they had arrived spiritually (scholars speak of 'over-realized eschatology': the Corinthians thought that they had progressed a long way in their experience of the eschatological life of heaven, when actually they were only experiencing what Paul elsewhere calls 'the first instalment' through the Spirit! (2 Corinthians 1.22, 5.5; Ephesians 1.14));
- a Greek world where human wisdom and rhetoric were especially esteemed, where pagan religion and morality were strong, and where the physical body was seen by many as spiritually unimportant;
- divisions between socially powerful rich people on the one hand and poor people on the other, including in the Christian community;
- other Christian leaders, notably Apollos, coming to Corinth after Paul; and
- normal human sinfulness –

given all this, what happened in Corinth is intelligible. It is not hard to see many parallels in the later history of the Church. Paul responds to the Corinthians with a whole range of arguments: he affirms their spirituality, but corrects their super-spirituality and emphasizes love; he affirms the goodness of creation and the body; above all he points to Jesus Christ, his cross and resurrection, as the benchmark of all true Christianity.

NOTE ON THE SIZE OF THE CHURCH

An interesting question raised by 1 Corinthians is how large the church was in Corinth. Again a video camera would help us! Some have argued that if the whole church met for a common meal, then the congregation must have been quite small, perhaps between 40 and 80. However, this seems a very low estimate. Acts tells us that the Jerusalem church in the early days was thousands strong, and, although we are not given figures for the churches founded by Paul, the impression is that whereas some places like Athens saw few conversions, other places saw conversions in large numbers: thus Acts says that 'a great number of Jews and Gentiles believed' in Iconium (14.1), 'many Jews and [...] not a few Greek men' became Christians in Berea (17.12), 'many of the Corinthians believed and were baptized' (18.8) and that 'all the Jews and Greeks who lived in the province of Asia heard the word of the Lord' (19.10). Of course, it is not certain how many is implied by the word 'many', but the suggestion is of a large movement, not a tiny congregation. Paul and his team did not stay in centres like Corinth and Ephesus for years and win only a handful of converts; they made a big impression. This may be confirmed by the hostility that the Church aroused, both among Jews and among Gentiles, as for example in Ephesus, where the finances of the temple of Artemis, which was very big business, were being badly affected by Christian conversions.

Paul's letters do not make the situation much clearer, but there are indications again that the Christian movement was substantial. So, when Paul speaks of the Thessalonians being converted and of how the Lord's message rang out from them 'not only in Macedonia and Achaia – your faith in God has become known everywhere' (1 Thessalonians 1.8), it sounds like a major turning to Christ, not just a few individual conversions. The opposition to Paul and his message noted in both Galatians and 1 Thessalonians suggests that the Christian movement was making more than ripples, seriously disturbing the Jews in particular. In Paul's later letter to the Romans he greets a whole range of people, and members of their household, suggesting that Rome at least had many Christians; this does not surprise us if the expulsion of the Jews from Rome a few years before in AD 49 was provoked by the growth of the Christian church. Even the emperor knew about the Christians!

As for Corinth, the impression we get from 1 Corinthians is that many things were happening in the Christian community, all sorts of different views being represented. It is hard to imagine that as small a group as 50 or even 100 would have been so radically divided on so many matters; it is fairly hard to imagine the poor being so disgracefully neglected at the Lord's Supper with such modest numbers. The impression we get of their worship is that there were numerous people taking part, speaking in tongues or prophesying; there were women who were causing a stir by their involvement; there were people who did not speak in tongues.

As for Paul's references to people: he lists those whom he baptized, namely Crispus, Gaius and the family of Stephanas, but implies that these were very much the exception to his rule, and that there were a lot of others who became Christians under his ministry and whom others of his colleagues baptized (1 Corinthians 1.14–16). In addition there were probably a good number of people whom Apollos baptized. Paul also mentions Chloe's household (1.11), and Fortunatus and Achaicus, who with Stephanas seem to be leaders of the church (16.17).

Romans was probably written from Corinth just a few years later, and in 16.1 Paul refers to Phoebe, a deacon of the church in Cenchreae, the port of Corinth, and says that she was a great support to 'many'. In the same chapter he refers to people who were with him: Timothy, Lucius, Jason and Sosipater, 'my relatives'; Tertius, who wrote the letter; Gaius, 'whose hospitality I and the whole church here enjoy'; Erastus, who is the city's director of public works; and 'our brother Quartus' (16.21–4). How many of these people were residents of Corinth and how many were in Paul's team is difficult to say, but in Romans alone we have ten named people (including Paul) who were in Corinth when Paul was writing, either colleagues of Paul or leaders of the church. It seems most unlikely that they comprised a quarter of the Sunday congregation! It seems probable that the church in Corinth had several hundred members, even if they did not all gather every Sunday in one place.

14 What does 1 Corinthians tell us about Paul and Jesus?

When it comes to 1 Corinthians we do not need a detective (or a sniffer dog!) to find out that Paul had taught the Corinthians a lot about Jesus. He tells us openly that he did so.

The resurrection

For example, in the passage we have just been discussing about the resurrection of the dead, Paul says:

> I want to remind you of the gospel I preached to you, which you received. [. . .] I passed on to you as of first importance what I also received, that Christ died for our sins according to the Scriptures, that he was buried, that he was raised on the third day according to the Scriptures, and that he appeared to Peter and then to the Twelve. After that, he appeared to more than five hundred of the brothers at the same time, most of whom are still living, though some have fallen asleep. Then he appeared to James, then to all the apostles, and last of all he appeared to me also, as to one abnormally born. For I am the least of the apostles[.]' (15.1–9)

Here we notice three things straight away:

1. Paul quite specifically says that the good news as he preached it has the story of Jesus at its heart; specifically he says that he passed on traditions of Jesus' death and resurrection to the Corinthians.
2. He says that he also 'received' them, which arguably takes us right back to the time of his conversion in the early 30s.
3. 'Receiving' and 'passing on' are probably technical terms such as were used by the Jewish rabbis to refer to the systematic teaching and learning of traditions.

So Paul gave great importance in his preaching of the gospel to the death and resurrection of Jesus, which is, of course, exactly what Matthew, Mark, Luke and John do in their accounts of Jesus.

But did Paul know any of the detailed stories narrated in the gospels? From his brief references to the death and burial of Jesus, we cannot prove that he did; in preaching the good news he might simply have told the Corinthians that Jesus died and was buried, without describing any of the circumstances. But this seems unlikely: in 1 Corinthians 15 he is obviously summarizing, and focusing on, the one point that is at issue – namely the question of resurrection. So he mentions Jesus' death and burial, since they led to the resurrection, but he does not bother to describe them, let alone what happened earlier in Jesus' life leading up to his death. Even so, his reference to Jesus dying 'according to the Scriptures' fits in with the gospel accounts, which make all sorts of connections between Jesus' death and the Old Testament (e.g. Mark 15.24 : Psalm 22.19; Mark 15.34 : Psalm 22.2, etc.), and his reference to Jesus' burial is interesting, since his argument does not demand such a reference, whereas the gospels quite deliberately describe how he was buried (Matthew 27.57–61; Mark 15.42–7; Luke 23.50–6; John 19.38–42).

When Paul comes to the resurrection, extra detail does arrive in the form of a list of witnesses to whom Jesus appeared. Paul agrees with the gospels that Jesus not only rose from the dead, but that he was seen by various people.

So is this a case of Paul demonstrating unequivocally his familiarity with the stories of Jesus, as we find them in the gospels? It is not quite as simple as that. Paul clearly does know about Jesus' resurrection and his resurrection appearances, and that is significant. But some people have argued that Paul actually undermines the gospels' version of the resurrection story: first, because he has a different list of witnesses from what we find in the gospels; second, because he does not refer to the women finding the tomb empty; and third, because he lists himself with the witnesses of the resurrected Jesus, showing that he thought of the resurrection in visionary terms, not in terms of an empty tomb and the physical body being raised.

However, these arguments are quite unpersuasive for the following reasons:

- Paul's list does overlap with the gospel accounts, especially with Luke's, since Luke refers to Jesus appearing to Peter and to the twelve on Easter Day (Luke 24.34–6).

- Paul's list is surely selective, not exhaustive: he says that Jesus appeared to:
  - Peter and the twelve;
  - 500 'brothers' who saw Jesus on one occasion;
  - James and all the apostles;
  - and then to himself as a late apostle.

Paul's selection is almost self-explanatory: he mentions the two biggest figures in the early church, Peter and James (Jesus' brother, who became leader of the Jerusalem church); he refers to the two major groups of which they were a part, the twelve and the wider group of apostles; and he refers to one other appearance – the one to 500 people at once. We may guess that he chose this because it was especially remarkable with such a large number involved. In addition he refers to himself, because this was especially important to him personally, and because it related to the controversial question of his apostleship. As we have seen, some wanted to put Paul down; he insisted that God had given him a position comparable to that of the twelve and the apostles and even to that of Peter and of James.

In Acts 1.3 there is reference to Jesus appearing to people many times over a period of forty days; the author of Luke and Acts evidently selected just a few of these to mention, and we may be confident that Paul did as well.

Paul is also very selective in that he only mentions the appearances (including his own) without describing them; it is unlikely that he knew only the fact that these appearances occurred. He probably knew the relevant stories, but in the context of 1 Corinthians 15 he is simply reminding his readers of stories already told, not retelling them.

- His failure to mention the women finding the tomb empty proves nothing. Some have suggested that it reflects the (lamentable) distrust of women's testimony in the ancient world; more probably it reflects again the summary nature of Paul's account. He chooses to mention the appearances of Jesus, which carry much more weight as evidence than the finding of an empty tomb. Not that Paul is ignorant of the empty tomb: his specific comment that Jesus 'was buried' followed by 'he was raised on the third day' could only suggest that the buried body had been raised. Most of the Jews who believed in life after death, in particular the Pharisees, believed in bodily resurrection, not just in the survival of the spirit or soul; Paul's subsequent discussion of the nature of the resurrection body shows that he believed that too (15.35–44; cf. Philippians 3.21).

- Paul's listing of himself with the witnesses of Jesus' resurrection does not show that he saw all the resurrection appearances as visionary. Although he clearly viewed his experience of the risen Christ as comparable theologically to the experiences of other apostles who saw Jesus, he quite openly admits that he was in a special category, speaking of himself as one 'abnormally born' (15.8). By this he may mean that he was a late entry to the privileged group of those who witnessed the resurrection, or that he was a surprising entry (since he had persecuted the church). Whatever the exact force of his words, his recognition that he was different in some respects means that we cannot reason confidently that Paul's experience was a vision and therefore he must have believed the other resurrection appearances to have been the same.

In any case, the argument about Paul's listing of his experience with the other resurrection appearances might lead us to exactly the opposite conclusion. Suppose Paul saw the resurrection appearances of Peter, James and others as more than visions. Might he then not have seen his own experience similarly? The case for this is good. 1 Corinthians 15 makes clear that Paul believed the resurrection appearances (to have lasted only for a limited time and to have been important in authenticating apostolic ministry. Neither of these points fits comfortably with a purely visionary interpretation, since visions of the Lord have been a feature of Christian experience throughout the ages (not just in the immediate post-resurrection period), and such visions do not convey apostolic authority to those who receive them. But the two points fit in well with the gospel narratives of the resurrection and notably with those of Luke and Acts. The gospels and Acts suggest that the resurrection appearances took place over forty days (until the ascension), that they were much more tangible experiences than even vivid visions – they saw and heard Jesus with their physical eyes and ears – and that they were to the apostles in particular (cf. Acts 1.1–11, 22; Luke 24.36–53). It makes good sense to surmise that Paul knew the stories of the resurrection in something like this form. It is also entirely feasible that Paul considered himself to have 'seen the Lord', not just in the way that people over the ages have seen the Lord in visions or dreams, but in a way comparable (though not identical) to that experienced by Peter and the others. If Acts is correct in saying that Paul was blinded on the Damascus Road, we can understand that he might have regarded his meeting with Jesus as much more than a vision in the mind.

We conclude that in 1 Corinthians 15 Paul is not just reproducing the stories of the resurrection as we find them in the gospels; he is an independent witness. But he is an independent witness to the resurrection story, whose account fits very well with the gospel narratives.

The Lord's Supper

As well as telling them about Jesus' death, burial and resurrection, Paul also told the Corinthians about his Last Supper with his disciples. Thus in 11.23–5 he says: 'I received from the Lord what I also passed on to you: the Lord Jesus, on the night he was betrayed, took bread, and when he had given thanks he broke it and said, "This is my body, which is for you; do this in remembrance of me." In the same way, after supper he took the cup, saying, "This cup is the new covenant in my blood; do this, whenever you drink it, in remembrance of me." '

Here we have the same language about learning and passing on tradition as we had with the resurrection, and in this case the wording is very close to the gospels. In particular it is very close to the account in Luke's gospel. (Matthew and Mark have Jesus say: 'This is my blood of the covenant, which is poured out for many' (Matthew 26.28; Mark 14.24); most manuscripts of Luke have 'This cup is the new covenant in my blood' (22.20) – the same thought but put slightly differently.)

This is further unambiguous evidence that Paul taught people about Jesus. Again we cannot prove exactly what he taught them. In 1 Corinthians he is not rehearsing everything, but just reminding them of what they already knew, and drawing their attention to a particular point – in this case that the supper is 'proclaiming the Lord's death', as Jesus made clear in his words about his body and his blood. However, the way Paul begins his reminder – 'on the night that he was betrayed' – suggests that they knew the story of how Jesus was betrayed as well as the story of the Last Supper. According to the gospels Jesus was arrested in the Garden of Gethsemane. When we looked at Galatians we wondered if Paul's use of 'Abba' reflected knowledge of the Gethsemane story; if so, this would certainly fit in with the evidence from 1 Corinthians. Other evidence might possibly point in the same direction: in Romans 8, for example, Paul speaks of the Christian *'crying* Abba', and also of the conflict between Spirit and flesh and of weakness in prayer; in the Gethsemane story Jesus urges the disciples to pray, and says 'the spirit is willing, but the flesh is weak' (e.g. Mark 14.38). There could possibly be a connection.

If we are right that Paul taught the Corinthians about Jesus' betrayal and the Last Supper and also about the resurrection appearances of Jesus, then it seems entirely likely that he told them the story of the crucifixion as well; he did not just tell them that Jesus 'died [. . .] and was buried', but he will have told them how it happened. This is what we suspected when we looked at Paul's comment to the Galatians about Jesus being 'portrayed as crucified' (3.1) and about the reference to the 'stigmata' (6.17). We might perhaps add the evidence of Colossians 2.14, which refers to Christ 'nailing to the cross' the bond of condemnation that stands against us as sinners; is this an allusion to the gospel story of Pilate nailing the charge 'king of the Jews' above Jesus' head? This cannot be proved, but is a possibility.

NOTE ON THE BODY OF CHRIST

This note to our discussion of the Lord's Supper relates to Paul's teaching about the Church as a body (e.g. in 1 Corinthians 12; Romans 12). Scholars have discussed at great length the origin of Paul's powerful picture of the Church. One possibility is that Paul 'received' this idea from Jesus' words at the Last Supper. Without going into all the historical debates about the eucharist, we may say relatively uncontroversially that the Last Supper is an extremely powerful picture of Jesus giving himself to his disciples. He said: 'This is my body', and then gave the bread to his disciples to eat. The picture is of the disciple taking Jesus – taking his body and blood – into him- or herself.

Paul comments in 1 Corinthians 10.16–17: 'is not the cup of thanksgiving for which we give thanks a participation in the blood of Christ? And is not the bread that we break a participation in the body of Christ?' The word for 'participation' is *koinonia*, and means 'sharing'. In the eucharist we act out taking (or actually take) Christ's body into ourselves, and thus share in Christ's body. Paul goes on to say, 'Because there is one loaf, we, who are many, are one body, for we all partake of the one loaf' (10.17). There is an interesting transition here from the thought of the loaf being Jesus' body (pictorially, at least) to the thought of those who eat the loaf being one body. Does Paul believe that, as we receive the body in the eucharist and share in it, so we are now the body of Christ, having his life and Spirit within us? It is possible that this is Paul's subtle, but rewarding, train of thought. If this is right, then it illustrates how traditions of Jesus have greatly influenced Paul. On the other hand, it is possible that Paul's idea of the church fellowship as a body is just the use of a rather obvious, but very fruitful, parable from life.

Another suggestion is that Paul's conversion experience and, in particular, the words of the risen Jesus to him on that occasion, 'Why are you persecuting me?' (Acts 9.4), could have been a significant catalyst to his thinking about the identification of Christ with the Church.

Sexual relations

Some scholars think that the story of Jesus' death was well known and important in the early Church, but that the stories and teachings of Jesus' ministry were not. However, we move on to further evidence from 1 Corinthians which tells against this.

Divorce

In 1 Corinthians 7 Paul considers the view that spiritual Christians should not have sex and indeed that married Christians should separate from their partners. He rejects this idea on various grounds, and in particular he quotes Jesus: 'To the married I give this command (not I, but the Lord): A wife must not separate from her husband. But if she does, she must remain unmarried or else be reconciled to her husband. And a husband must not divorce his wife.' He then writes: 'To the rest I say this (I, not the Lord) . . .' (7.10–12).

The first thing to notice about this is how Paul makes it clear that he is quoting Jesus. His 'not I, but the Lord' is like an opening inverted comma, and his 'I say this (I, not the Lord)' is like a closing inverted comma. He is quoting Jesus.

The second thing to notice is that he regards Jesus' teaching as authoritative and above his own (though Paul does believe in his own apostolic authority!).

The third thing to notice is that Paul's words, though not word for word the same as those of Jesus, are very close to the teaching of Jesus as it is found in Mark 10.1–12 and Matthew 19.1–9. Jesus in these passages is asked for his opinion about the controversial issue of divorce. He refers his hearers back to the story in Genesis 2 of God creating Adam and Eve to be 'one flesh', and then makes two slightly different points, the second clarifying the first:

1. 'Therefore, what God has joined together, let man not separate';
2. 'Anyone who divorces his wife and marries another woman commits adultery against her. And if she divorces her husband and marries another man, she commits adultery.'

What is noticeable about this is that Paul in 1 Corinthians 7 uses exactly this pattern:

1. a general statement against divorce using almost exactly the same phrase, 'not to separate', and then
2. a particular statement ruling out remarriage 'if' separation takes place.

Paul talks about the wife before the husband, and this, as we saw, is one of the indications that it may have been spiritual women who were advocating sexual abstinence. But it is in any case clear that he has the gospel story in mind. This is striking evidence for the importance of Jesus' teaching for Paul, because it is explicit and unambiguous.

Celibacy

In the same context in 1 Corinthians there are other, more ambiguous clues pointing in the same direction. Thus immediately before his teaching on divorce, Paul comments on Christian celibacy, recommending it; but he says that it is not for everyone: 'each man has his own gift from God: one has this gift, another has that' (7.7). Later in the chapter he gives some of his reasons for valuing celibacy, explaining how marriage and family life can bring troubles and how the unmarried person can give undistracted attention to 'the Lord's affairs' (vv. 28, 32).

All of this is reminiscent of what Jesus says in Matthew's gospel straight after his teaching on divorce. The disciples have responded to Jesus' strict teaching on divorce with the words 'then it is better not to marry'. Jesus replies, 'Not everyone can accept this word, but only those to whom it has been given. For some are eunuchs because they were born that way; others were made that way by men, and others have made themselves eunuchs because of the kingdom of heaven. The one who can accept this should accept this' (19.11–12). The references to 'eunuchs' may seem rather obscure to us but, when Jesus refers to those who 'have made themselves eunuchs for the sake of the kingdom of heaven', he is probably referring to those who 'have renounced marriage' for the sake of the kingdom (so the NIV translation). Jesus sees this as something good, but not for everyone; it is only for those 'to whom it has been given'. This is exactly Paul's position in 1 Corinthians 7. He sees celibacy as a gift for some only, and in explaining why he may well be echoing Jesus' teaching.

It is an interesting possibility that the 'spiritual' Corinthians may have appealed to the same story, but they could have read Jesus' words about 'eunuchs' as suggesting that all really spiritual Christians ought to embrace celibacy – 'the one who can accept this should accept this'. Other stories and sayings of Jesus could have influenced them, including Jesus' vivid statements about disciples needing to 'hate' their family members (e.g. Matthew 12.46–50), and in particular Jesus' discussion of resurrection with the Sadducees (Matthew 22.23–33; Mark 12.18–27; Luke 20.27–40).

In that story the Sadducees wished to disprove all ideas of resurrection, and so put to Jesus the imaginary case of a woman who had seven husbands, all of whom died in turn; 'at the resurrection', they asked Jesus, 'whose wife will she be?' Jesus' response to this ingenious question is: 'the people of this age

151

marry and are given in marriage. But those who are considered worthy of taking part in that age and in the resurrection from the dead will neither marry nor be given in marriage, and they can no longer die; for they are like the angels. They are God's children, since they are children of the resurrection' (Luke 20.35–6). Did the Corinthians know this story of Jesus? We cannot prove that they did, but it is not at all hard to see how they might have reasoned from it to their advocacy of Christian celibacy. They could have deduced, logically enough, that the spiritually superior way to live – the way of heaven – was celibacy. If they were expecting Jesus to return soon, then this surely was the way to live in preparing for his coming. If some of them thought, as seems to be the case, that they were already in the new age through the Spirit (speaking in tongues of angels!), then presumably they should no longer go on being married and sexually active. Perhaps some of their doubts about the resurrection came also from the same saying of Jesus; after all, if we are already God's children, raised spiritually with Christ, and if God's children no longer die, then how exactly does any other sort of resurrection fit into the picture?

Luke's version of the story lends itself to this suggestion particularly clearly, since the references to 'not dying' and to 'children of the resurrection' are in Luke, not Matthew or Mark; but whichever version they knew, the suggestion is attractive.

Another story of Jesus that may have been used by the 'spiritual' Corinthians is the story of Jesus visiting the home of the two sisters Mary and Martha (Luke 10.38–42). Martha is preparing the meal for Jesus, and is feeling hard-pressed and hard done by; Mary is sitting at Jesus' feet listening to his teaching, i.e. in the role of a disciple. Martha complains about Mary, but Jesus replies, 'Martha, Martha, you are worried and upset about many things, but only one thing is needed. Mary has chosen what is better, and it will not be taken away from her' (10.41–2).

The story is remarkable in its portrayal of Jesus' positive view of women: women would not usually be welcomed as disciples by Jewish rabbis. It is one of the stories which may have contributed to the positive view of women in the Church and in ministry, which we noticed when looking at Galatians 3.28: in Christ 'there is no male and female'. But it is also a story that could have encouraged the liberated 'spiritual' women of Corinth to argue that celibate discipleship was preferable to domesticity: Jesus after all described Mary as choosing the better part.

This suggestion that they may have cited the story of Mary and Martha is not just speculation without any basis: there is some evidence in 1 Corinthians that may support it. The evidence comes in Paul's discussion of the unmarried state, where he contrasts the distractedness of the married with the unmarried, who are able to give undivided devotion to the Lord (7.32–5). Some of the vocabulary that Paul uses here, e.g. 'worried', 'devoted' (originally the Greek word meant something like 'sitting well beside'), 'undistracted', is unusual for him, but similar to that found in the story of Mary and Martha.

Of course, one other aspect of the story of Jesus which will very likely have encouraged the Corinthians who were advocating a celibate lifestyle was Jesus' own celibacy. After all, did not Paul advocate imitating Christ and himself as the follower of Christ (1 Corinthians 4.16, 11.1)?

We can't prove that Paul and the Corinthians were appealing to stories of Jesus for their views about celibacy, but it is a plausible hypothesis, especially since (*a*) we have seen that in 1 Corinthians 7 Paul is certainly appealing to Jesus on the subject of divorce and (*b*) several of the stories of Jesus to which we have referred, such as that of Mary and Martha, are recorded in Luke's gospel – a gospel which seems to have come out of Pauline circles (as Acts, the follow-up volume to Luke, suggests, with its strong focus on Paul).

Prostitution

It is not just the advocates of celibacy in Corinth who may have been quoting Jesus' teaching. It may seem surprising, but it is possible that the men going to prostitutes were doing the same. We have seen that they were probably justifying their actions by arguing that Paul taught them that Christians were free from the law: 'all things are permissible', they were saying (6.12). But were they also appealing to the teaching of Jesus? This is suggested by the way Paul describes their view: 'Food for the stomach and the stomach for food. But God will destroy both' (6.13). We may wonder what the food and stomach have to do with the question of prostitution. Is the context one of orgiastic meals, with sex thrown in? Possibly. But it is also possible that the Corinthians were taking what Jesus said about food and applying it to sex.

To understand this point, we need to recall a story of Jesus in Mark and Matthew (Mark 7.1–23; Matthew 15.1–20). Jesus' disciples, according to the gospels, caused offence to the Pharisees and scribes by 'eating food with hands that were unclean, that is, unwashed' (Mark 7.3). Jesus replied by attacking his opponents' inverted priorities, and then commented, 'Nothing outside a person can make him unclean by going into him. Rather, it is what comes out of a man that makes him unclean' (Mark 7.15). When pressed by his disciples to clarify this he comments: 'Don't you see that nothing that enters a man from the outside can make him "unclean"? For it doesn't go into his heart but into his stomach, and then out of his body' (7.18–19a). Mark then adds, 'In saying this, Jesus declared all foods clean' (7.19b).

Mark's last comment, about Jesus declaring all foods clean (literally 'cleansing all foods'), is Mark's interpretation of Jesus' saying: Mark understands Jesus as meaning that the Old Testament food laws are no longer binding, at least on his Gentile readers. Paul seems to have reasoned in the same way. In Romans 14.14 he comments that 'In the Lord Jesus I am persuaded that no food is unclean'. The phrase 'in the Lord Jesus I am persuaded' here could simply mean something like 'as a Christian I believe', but it seems more likely that the reference to 'the Lord' is like his reference to 'the word of the Lord' about the dead in 1 Thessalonians 4.15 and like his references to 'the Lord's' words on the Last Supper and on divorce in 1 Corinthians 11.23 and 7.10. In other words Paul is referring back to Jesus' teaching. It seems probable that in Romans 14.14 he is recalling Jesus' teaching on cleanness and uncleanness, and probably doing exactly what Mark was doing, i.e. interpreting Jesus' saying as spelling the end of the old laws about clean and unclean food. This was something very important for Paul, because of his disputes with the Jewish Christians who wanted to maintain the Old Testament law intact.

It is entirely likely, given its importance for him, that Paul will have passed on this teaching to the Corinthians (cf. also Colossians 2.21–2). He will have taught them about Christians being free from the law, and quoted Jesus' teaching in that connection. What he will not, presumably, have anticipated is that some of the Corinthians would seize on his teaching about Christian freedom, and in particular on the idea of 'nothing coming into a person from outside' making a person unclean, to justify sexual licence. After all, in the gospel story itself the question of food is linked to the question of hand-washing, and it was convenient logic for the Corinthians to apply the teaching about food to another bodily function, i.e. sex. Jesus' comment about food going into the stomach and so passing on could well have led the Corinthians to say 'Food for the stomach, the stomach for food. God will destroy both', and then to argue that sex is a similarly harmless physical function of the body which has no relevance to the heart and the spirit; they are what matter, as Jesus said.

This logic may seem perverse to us, but we are familiar enough in the modern world with people interpreting the Bible perversely to suit their own views! The Corinthians had more excuse than modern interpreters, since the working-out of Christian living free from the Jewish law in a pagan world was something new then, and there was a logic both in the spiritual asceticism of some, and the sexual freedom of others.

Paul has to argue with both positions. What is interesting in this reconstruction of things is that both he and his opponents are quoting the teaching and traditions of Jesus. He had taught them what Jesus had said about all sorts of things, including marriage, divorce, celibacy, the kingdom of God, and cleanness; they took this teaching on board, but interpreted some of it in ways that Paul rejected; he then has to correct their interpretations. In doing so, he uses a variety of arguments, some of which draw further on the teaching of Jesus. Thus against the libertines he uses Jesus' teaching about the righteousness of the kingdom of God (1 Corinthians 6.9–11; see further below); he also reminds them of the resurrection of the body of Jesus, thus dealing a knock-out blow to their ideas about the unimportance and transience of the body (6.14). Against the ascetics he quotes Jesus' teaching on divorce – Jesus told married couples to stick together and not to separate; on celibacy Paul brings out the point (made by Jesus) about celibacy being a gift of God. In addressing both the libertines and the ascetics

(1 Corinthians 6.16, 7.4) he refers to the creation story of man and woman becoming 'one flesh' (Genesis 2.24), which Jesus also quoted in his discussion on divorce (Matthew 19.5). In this case Paul need not have been influenced by Jesus, since he was so familiar with the Old Testament himself.

However, it is quite clear that the stories and sayings of Jesus were common ground for both Paul and the Corinthian Christians, and that they were seen to have great authority, even though their interpretation was debated. (It may be significant that, where Mark has Jesus saying that 'nothing that enters a person from outside can make him unclean' (7.16), Matthew has 'What goes into a person's mouth does not make him unclean' (15.10). Did Matthew reword the saying to avoid the Corinthians' licentious misunderstanding?)

Apostleship

Paul appeals explicitly to Jesus' teaching on divorce, but also to his teaching on apostleship – in 1 Corinthians 9.14.

The context is Paul discussing the Christian attitude to food offered to idols. Paul's view is that the Christian may eat any food, for 'the earth is the Lord's, and everything in it' (10.26; also, as we saw, he believed that 'in the Lord Jesus' nothing is unclean: Romans 14.14). In that respect he is on the side of the 'stronger' Christians in Corinth who believed that it was all right to eat food sold or prepared by pagans who will have offered it in sacrifice to idols. But Paul balances that affirmation with a very strong argument that the Christian should not cause 'weaker' brothers or sisters to go against their conscience. It is better to sacrifice 'my' freedom than to cause someone else to stumble in their faith.

The rights and freedom of an apostle

Paul illustrates this point with a discussion of his own apostleship. Significantly, he starts by asking the questions: 'Am I not free? Am I not an apostle? Have I not seen the Lord?' (9.1). He then explains that he is indeed an apostle with all the rights of an apostle, but he has sacrificed those rights and his freedom for the sake of the gospel. In particular he has sacrificed his apostolic right to financial support, and instead worked with his own hands to support himself.

But where does this idea of apostolic rights come from? The answer – or an important part of the answer – is that 'the Lord commanded that those who preach the gospel should receive their living by the gospel' (9.14). The strong probability is that Paul is here quoting from Jesus' commissioning of his disciples, because when Jesus sent them out on mission he told them to take nothing for the journey, but to accept hospitality when it was offered. In Luke, when Jesus sends the seventy-two out on mission, he tells them to find a well-disposed household, and then to 'stay in that house, eating and drinking whatever they give you, for the worker deserves his wages' (10.7; cf. Matthew 10.10).

More specifically, the following observations favour the linking of Paul's and Jesus' teaching here:

- Paul says he is quoting Jesus.
- The saying of Jesus from the mission discourse suits Paul's purposes, in that it makes the point about gospel workers being supported.
- The context of the saying is Paul talking about apostleship and about himself as a real apostle like the others; and the saying of Jesus appears in his instructions to those whom he is 'sending out' (*apostello*, the verb corresponding to the word 'apostle': Matthew 10.5, 16; Mark 6.7; Luke 9.2, 10.1).
- Paul does not quote word for word the saying of Jesus about the labourer being 'worthy of his wages', but he does go on to talk about his 'wages' consisting (paradoxically) of making his gospel free of charge 1 Corinthians 9.17–18).
- Paul speaks of those who 'preach' the gospel, and this is precisely what the disciples of Jesus are sent out to do (Matthew 10.7; Mark 6.12; Luke 9.2).
- Paul speaks of having the 'right to food and drink' (9.3), which is precisely what the disciples are told by Jesus to accept (Luke 10.7).
- Paul talks about his 'authority' (or 'right') as an apostle (1 Corinthians 9.4, 18), and Jesus gives his disciples 'authority' in their mission (Matthew 10.1; Luke 9.1).

This accumulation of evidence adds up to a very strong case that Paul has in mind the saying about the labourer being worthy of his wages, when he speaks of the preacher getting his living by the gospel. But it also suggests that Paul was familiar not just with this one saying, but with the whole mission discourse of Jesus.

When looking at Galatians, we noticed that there Paul seems to know Jesus' restriction of the mission of the twelve to Israel: 'go only to the lost sheep of the house of Israel' (Matthew 10.5). This is found in Matthew's version of the mission discourse, and is therefore another piece of evidence that that discourse was known to Paul. Admittedly we are again making links between Paul and different gospel accounts – the restriction to Israel is in Matthew, the comment about eating and drinking is in Luke (though Matthew significantly speaks of the 'labourer being worthy of his food'!: 10.10). But this is no problem: if Paul and the gospel writers are all drawing on early traditions of Jesus and not solely on one common source, then we would expect a complicated pattern of agreement and disagreement, which is precisely what we find.

Forgoing the rights of an apostle

We have not yet commented on the fact that Paul's argument about his willingness to forgo his rights as an apostle had a problematic side to it. He knew, and indeed reminds the Corinthians, that the Lord had commanded apostles to get their living by the gospel; but he was not doing that! It may be that this was one of the complaints that his detractors had levelled against him: how could he claim to be a true apostle of Jesus, and not do as Jesus said? Was this one of the reasons he was accused of being inferior to Apollos, not to mention other apostles like Peter, all of whom willingly accepted hospitality?

Paul's reply is not to doubt the Lord's command, but to explain that there were good gospel reasons to renounce this 'right' or 'authority'. Thus:

- As we have noted, he argues, paradoxically, that his 'wages' or his reward lie in making the gospel free of charge. Paul could here be echoing Jesus' words: 'Freely you have received, freely give' (from the mission discourse in Matthew 10.8).
- He also speaks out strongly against 'offending' one's Christian brother (1 Corinthians 8.13; Romans 14.21; cf. 2 Corinthians

11.29): the word for 'offend', *skandalizo* in Greek, is helpfully translated 'cause to stumble'. It is not a common word in secular Greek, but it is an important word in Jesus' teaching, according to the gospels. For instance, Jesus warns very vividly and strongly that 'if anyone causes one of these little ones who believe in me to stumble, it would be better for him to be thrown into the sea with a large millstone tied around his neck' (Mark 9.42; see also Mark 9.43–7; Matthew 18.6–8, 17.27; Luke 17.2). It seems likely that this teaching of Jesus lies behind Paul's concern for the 'weak', and his willingness to forgo his rights for the sake of others.

- He goes on to speak of 'making himself a slave to everyone, to win the more' (1 Corinthians 9.19). The language here is strikingly reminiscent of Jesus' instructions to his disciples in Mark 10, where Jesus comments on the disciples' quest for greatness, and invites them to the way of service: 'whoever wants to be first must be slave of all. For even the Son of Man did not come to be served, but to serve, and to give his life a ransom for many' (43–5). The idea of 'a ransom for many' is not a million miles away from Paul's words about 'winning [or 'gaining'] the more', and it seems possible, if not probable, that Paul has Jesus' words about being a slave and a servant in mind when he explains his ministry. It is also worth observing that in several of his letters Paul specifically calls himself 'a slave of Jesus Christ' – a striking and significant title to use of himself (Romans 1.1; Philippians 1.1; Titus 1.1; cf. Galatians 1.10).

Scholars have noticed how the sophists of Paul's day had 'disciples', but Paul never speaks of his converts or members of his congregations as his disciples. They are 'brothers' or, less frequently, 'dear children'. It seems likely that Jesus' teaching about servant-leadership and about Christians being members of Christ's family has influenced Paul, and that this is also reflected in the lack of evidence of strict hierarchical leadership in his churches (cf. Matthew 23.8–11; Mark 3.34–5; Luke 17.10).

If Paul is balancing one saying of Jesus (about the labourer's wages) against others (about not causing others to stumble and about humble service), then that shows once again how important the teaching of Jesus was, and how questions of interpretation were as significant then as now. Paul, notably, does not subscribe to a wooden, literalistic interpretation of Jesus' saying about the labourer's wages, but interprets it intelligently in the light of Jesus' central teaching on service. We saw possible clues in Galatians that Paul knew this passage (see our discussion of Galatians 2.6–9, 5.13 and 6.2 in Chapter 7). In Galatians 2.6–9 he showed some irritation with his opponents' appeal to the 'pillars'; for him Jesus' words to James, John and the other apostles about being a servant needed to be remembered. According to 1 Corinthians 9 he tried to put those words into action in his own life, forgoing the rights and freedoms of an apostle.

Paul and Apollos

Before leaving the matter of apostleship and servanthood, we need to be reminded of Paul's discussion of himself and Apollos in the opening chapters of 1 Corinthians. There are various possible echoes of Jesus' teaching here: in particular, Paul insists that he and Apollos ought to be regarded as 'servants of Christ and as those entrusted with the secret things of God', who will give account to 'the Lord' when he comes and who will then receive their 'praise' from God (4.1–5). This sounds very much like the parables about the Lord's coming, and in particular like the parable of the steward (Matthew 24.45–51; Luke 12.42–6). The parable of the talents, with its reference to the master praising his 'good and faithful' servants (Matthew 25.19–30; Luke 19.12–27), could also have been in Paul's mind, and may lie behind Paul's comments in chapter 12 about the Spirit giving different gifts to different people (1 Corinthians 12.7–11). That Paul was familiar with such eschatological parables of Jesus was clear when we examined 1 Thessalonians in Chapter 10.

But going back to Paul and Apollos, Paul compares himself and Apollos to farmers working in 'God's field', an agricultural imagery familiar in Jesus' parables, though not necessarily derived from that (1 Corinthians 3.5–9; cf. Matthew 13; Mark 4; Luke 8). He speaks also of them as builders in God's building, and comments on Jesus Christ being the only true Christian foundation. We recall Jesus' parable of the wise and foolish builders at the end of the Sermon on the Mount; significantly, the wise builder is the person who 'hears these words of mine and does them' (Matthew 7.24–7; Luke 6.47–9).

In Matthew's gospel Jesus speaks of his words being the only sound foundation, but also of the Church being built on Peter (Matthew 16.16–20); we suggested that Paul may show knowledge of this tradition of Peter's primacy in Galatians, but he is unhappy about those who exalt Peter at his (Paul's) expense. In 1 Corinthians 3 he emphasizes Jesus as the only foundation in the context of discussing the Corinthian adulation of human leaders, including Peter: the Corinthians must not exalt human leaders, who are mere servants, instead of exalting Jesus, who is Lord of Paul, Apollos and Peter (3.22).

In the same discussion of building, Paul refers to the Corinthians as 'God's temple', and warns against those who would 'destroy' it (3.16). This remarkable teaching, which we examined in Chapter 7, here comes to light once more. We suggested that a likely background was Jesus' own teaching about the destruction and rebuilding of the temple, in connection with his own death. If the Church is now the temple of God, the priority is not to destroy (3.16–17), but to 'build it up', this being a key concept for Paul in his discussion of spiritual gifts in chapters 12–14 (see e.g. 14.4, 5, 12).

Baptism and the kingdom of God

So far in this chapter we have noted a remarkable amount of strong and explicit evidence showing how important the sayings and stories of Jesus were for Paul and the Corinthians; we have also seen some less certain but possible echoes. The list of possibles can easily be extended.

We have mentioned the baptism texts in 1 Corinthians 1.15, 6.11 and 12.12–13, and suggested that Paul could have had the baptism of Jesus in mind as the model of Christian baptism. The expression in 12.13, 'we were all baptized by one Spirit', is reminiscent of the words of John the Baptist when he predicted the coming of one who would 'baptize you in the Holy Spirit' (e.g. Mark 1.8).

We have also mentioned before some of the texts referring to the kingdom of God. In 6.9–11 Paul comments on how the 'unrighteous will not inherit the kingdom of God'. We observed how the use of the phrase 'kingdom of God' and the association of the kingdom with righteousness may well go back to Jesus.

Earlier Paul comments that 'the kingdom of God is not a matter of talk but of power' (4.20). Paul is here speaking of Christian leaders, whose authenticity is seen in their action, not their talk. We are reminded of the gospel picture of the kingdom of God coming in power – evidenced in Jesus' miracles and in the miracles of the apostles whom he sends out. Paul does not talk a lot about miracles, his or anyone else's. But he does speak in 1 Corinthians 2.4 about his message coming not with wise and persuasive words, but 'with a demonstration of the Spirit's power'; he does speak of 'authority' in connection with his discussion of apostleship in 1 Corinthians 9; and then in 2 Corinthians 12.12 he is quite clear about how 'the things that mark an apostle – signs, wonders and miracles – were done among you with great perseverance'. This is rather clear evidence that Paul knows about miracles being connected with apostles (see also Romans 15.19).

Faith, knowledge and charity

Another important text relating to miracles is 1 Corinthians 13.2, where Paul says, 'if I have a faith that can move mountains, but have not love, I am nothing' (v. 2). The reference to faith moving mountains sounds very like Jesus' teaching as found in Matthew 17.20: 'If you have faith as a mustard seed you will say to this mountain, "Move from here to there", and it will move' (cf. Luke 17.6 and Matthew 21.21/Mark 11.22–3). Admittedly Jesus in the gospels is recommending such faith, whereas Paul seems to be de-emphasizing it in favour of love. But in fact Paul is not denying the value of such faith. What he is saying is that the very greatest of spiritual achievements or powers, including mountain-moving faith, are useless without love – a message that the charismatic Corinthians badly needed to hear. It seems likely that Paul got this unusually vivid image of faith from Jesus, and that the Corinthians would have known its origin.

In the same context, Paul comments that 'if I have the gift of prophecy and can fathom all mysteries and all knowledge [...] but have not love, I am nothing' (v. 2). This was clearly a relevant word for the Corinthians, who so strongly emphasized prophecy and knowledge. But it may be that there is a further echo of Jesus here, since according to the gospels Jesus told his disciples that 'it has been given to you to know the mysteries of the kingdom of heaven/ God' (Matthew 13.11; Luke 8.10; cf. Mark 4.10). It is not difficult to imagine that the Corinthians knew this text, and claimed it for themselves. They believed that through the work of the Spirit they had the divine knowledge of which Jesus spoke. And they were very proud of it. Paul does not deny that the Corinthians have divinely given knowledge, but again he puts the gift in perspective: it is useless without love.

He goes on to say, 'If I give all my possessions to charity and surrender my body to be burned, but have not love, I gain nothing' (v. 3). What higher sacrifices could there be? The reference to giving 'all my possessions' sounds like another echo of Jesus, since this is precisely the challenge Jesus puts to the rich young ruler in the gospels (Matthew 19.21; Mark 10.21; Luke 18.22). In Luke's gospel the same challenge is directed to all the disciples (12.33).

We may conclude that in 1 Corinthians 13 Paul is recalling some of the most important examples of spirituality as taught by Jesus, but insisting on the absolute priority of love, which was, of course, the priority in Jesus' own teaching, as we saw earlier.

Wisdom and revelation

The suggestion that the Corinthians saw themselves as having the knowledge and revelation of which Jesus spoke may possibly be confirmed by 1 Corinthians 1—4, where Paul discusses wisdom and foolishness. The language Paul uses to discuss the Corinthians' ideas about wisdom and knowledge, including his reference to 'babes' (3.1), has reminded some scholars of Matthew 11.25–7/ Luke 10.21–2, where Jesus says: 'I praise you, Father, Lord of heaven and earth, because you have hidden these things from the wise and learned, and revealed them to babes. Yes, Father, for this was your good pleasure. All things have been committed to me by my Father. No one knows the Son except the Father, and no one knows the Father except the Son and those to whom the Son chooses to reveal him.' It seems possible that this passage was well known, and was important for the Corinthians, who were claiming spiritual wisdom and revelation.

It may well have been important for Paul too, though he sees the Corinthians' arrogance as a mark of worldly wisdom rather than of the secret gospel wisdom of Christ. The Old Testament and later Jewish writings spoke of God's wisdom in almost personal terms, as if she were a colleague working alongside God (e.g. Proverbs 8; Wisdom 7). Paul speaks of Christ as 'our wisdom', and there are a number of gospel passages in which Jesus associates himself with Old Testament wisdom (including Matthew 11.28–9; Luke 7.35, 11.31, 49).

The Sermon on the Mount

If the Corinthians saw themselves as God's sages, they may also have seen themselves as the blessed of Jesus' beatitudes. The Sermon on the Mount opens with Jesus blessing 'the poor' or the 'poor in spirit' and commenting that the kingdom of heaven is theirs; he goes on to speak of the hungry being filled (Matthew 5.3–10; Luke 6.20–3). Paul says to the Corinthians, with a good deal of irony, that 'Already you have all you want! Already you have become rich! You have become kings' (1 Corinthians 4.8). It seems possible that the charismatic Corinthians saw themselves precisely in those terms, as people already possessing the kingdom, already full of the Holy Spirit; they might have deduced this from the beatitudes of Jesus. But Paul suggests that there is an oddness about their conviction, since the apostles seem to be exactly the opposite: 'We are fools for Christ. We are weak [. . .] we are dishonoured [. . .] we go hungry and thirsty [. . .] we have become the scum of the earth, the refuse of the world' (4.10–13).

There are various other possible echoes of the Sermon on the Mount in Paul's letters, the most striking in Romans 12.14–17, where Paul's words about blessing and not cursing 'those who persecute you' and about not repaying evil for evil are strongly reminiscent of Jesus' words about loving even one's enemies. The enigmatic words in 2 Corinthians 1.17 about saying 'yes, yes' and 'no, no' sound a little like Matthew 5.37, but the connection is not particularly obvious, at least on the surface.

Church discipline

Paul's words in 1 Corinthians 5.3–5 about excluding an immoral member from the congregation have some interesting similarities to Jesus' words in Matthew 18.15–20 about dealing with a Christian who offends you. In both contexts the picture is of the church taking a decision to exclude someone, and in both there is a reference to the speaker being spiritually present: in Matthew 18 Jesus promises to be among his disciples in such a situation, and in 1 Corinthians 5.5 Paul talks about his spirit, with the power of the Lord Jesus, being present with the Corinthians. The resemblance is curious, but perhaps not accidental.

Adam and the Son of Man

One of Paul's most important theological ideas in 1 Corinthians is his designation of Jesus as the second Adam in chapter 15. An interesting question is whether Paul has been influenced in this by Jesus' teaching about himself as 'Son of Man'.

Son of Man seems to have been Jesus' favourite way of identifying himself: he doesn't refer to himself in the gospels as Messiah by preference, or very often as Son of God (though he does speak to God as Abba), but he uses the term Son of Man frequently. It is a Semitic phrase, typical of Hebrew and Aramaic, and it means literally human being. So Jesus in the gospels refers to himself frequently as 'the human being'.

Scholars have debated the significance of this at length. The clue that the gospel writers give us is their description of the Son of Man coming on the clouds of heaven, since this immediately evokes the description in Daniel 7 of 'one like a son of man [human being] coming on the clouds' (cf. Mark 13.26, 14.62; Daniel 7.13). In Daniel 7 this comes in a vision in which:

- Four terrible beasts appear first, evidently representing the pagan empires of the world;
- There is then a judgement scene before 'the ancient of days' (i.e. God), and the judgement that is delivered from God is the deposing or destroying of the beasts;
- Then 'one like a son of man', i.e. a human figure, is seen, and

165

the power and authority and kingdom that previously belonged to the beasts is now given to the human figure. This human figure represents 'the saints of the most high', in other words God's people (i.e. Israel in Daniel's terms).

If this was the background to Jesus' usage – interestingly Daniel 7 is in Aramaic, Jesus' own language – then we may suspect that Jesus used the expression of himself in order to say that God's salvation of Israel was coming through him; he was bringing 'the kingdom' to Israel. It was a fairly enigmatic way of saying this about himself, but that may have been part of the point, since Jesus did not wish to be turned into a popular Messiah.

Whether this was the background or not, one of the striking things about the expression Son of Man is that it is used very little of Jesus outside the gospels. We may guess that this is because it was a distinctly Semitic expression, not immediately meaningful when turned into Greek, but also because the first Christians preferred some more honorific title for Jesus than 'the human being'.

However, it is possible that Paul has been influenced by the expression, and that this contributed to his description of Jesus as the new 'Adam'. He compares Jesus and Adam in various contexts, and it is clearly an important concept to him (Romans 6, 1 Corinthians 15; and perhaps Philippians 2.5–11). He need not have been influenced by the term Son of Man; on the other hand, given its importance in the gospels it is entirely possible that he was.

A small piece of evidence that may point in that direction is in 1 Corinthians 15 itself, because in verses 25 and 26 Paul speaks of all things being put under Jesus' feet, quoting from Psalm 8.6. The psalm is about God as creator and man as his authoritative agent over creation, and it uses the phrase 'son of man' in verse 4. 'What is man that you are mindful of him, the son of man that you care for him?' There are unmistakable echoes in the psalm of the Genesis story of the creation of Adam, but Paul applies the psalm to Jesus. It is not impossible that the psalm influenced Jesus but, whether it did or not, there is no doubt that it influenced Paul, and it could be that Jesus' use of the expression Son of Man led Paul and others to think about Jesus as the Adamic figure of Psalm 8 (cf. Hebrews 2.6–9).

166

Paul may also have reflected on Daniel 7. Thus in 1 Corinthians 6, where he considers the scandal of Christians taking each other to the law courts, he says that such cases should be taken rather to 'the saints', and he says, 'Do you not know that the saints will judge the world?' (6.2). It seems quite possible that the background to this is Daniel 7.27, where the saints are given authority and rule; indeed the Daniel passage may lie behind Paul's regular use of the word 'saints' to refer to Christians (e.g. 1 Corinthians 1.2). (Another possible background to 1 Corinthians 6.2 is the saying of Jesus about the twelve judging the twelve tribes of Israel: Matthew 19.28; Luke 22.29–30.)

The Lord's return

The Corinthians, like the Thessalonians, were looking for the Lord's return. 'Maranatha' – come, O Lord – was their cry (1 Corinthians 16.22). We might imagine that they were taught much the same as the Thessalonians, and this assumption is borne out by the relatively brief description of the Lord's return in 1 Corinthians 15.51–2, where Paul speaks of those who 'sleep' being raised, of the sounding of the trumpet, and of the conquering of death. We saw also in our discussion of 1 Thessalonians that the reference to the 'present distress' in 1 Corinthians 7.26 could be an echo of Jesus' teaching.

Conclusion

1 Corinthians turns out to be packed with possible echoes of the teaching and stories of Jesus. Some of them are nothing more than vague possibilities, and our detective would not be impressed by them on their own (e.g. the Adam–Son of Man connection, the echoes of the Sermon on the Mount); some seem quite probable (e.g. the Mary–Martha story, the emphasis on service and not causing others to stumble, the comment about faith that moves mountains, etc.), and others are beyond dispute (e.g. the divorce saying, the rights of an apostle, the Last Supper and resurrection), because Paul labels them as such. The fact that Paul is so explicit in these last passages in referring to his passing on of traditions to the

Corinthians means that the 'probable' echoes begin to look highly probable, and the possibles look probable! There is a strong cumulative case, and there is a remarkable range of gospel stories and sayings that are possibly or probably attested in 1 Corinthians.

It is interesting to reflect that the echoes of Jesus in 1 Corinthians overlap a little with the echoes we detected in Galatians and the Thessalonian letters, but that to a large extent they are different. What is clear, as we have argued before, is that the selection of echoes in each letter is determined by the problems in the particular church. Thus in 1 Corinthians there is a specific focus on the Last Supper, because the Corinthians' eucharistic meals were a mess! There is a specific reference to the resurrection appearances, because resurrection was a debated issue in Corinth. The fact that Paul does not describe the crucifixion is not because he had not taught the Corinthians about it; he almost certainly had done so, but it was unnecessary to retell the story in the letter. It would have been wasted ink! It is salutary to reflect that, if the Corinthians had not had problems in their eucharists, we would have had no evidence at all that Paul knew or taught about the Last Supper in any of his churches. He does not need to mention it in his other letters. We conclude that silence does not prove ignorance – not at all. The references that we do have to the stories and sayings of Jesus are the tip of an iceberg that is mostly concealed from us.

PART 3
FINISHING THE STORY

15 And so on

Having followed Paul's footsteps with some care up to Ephesus, we are shortly going to leave him – not because his story came to an end in Ephesus, but for the sake of brevity and because we have already covered enough ground to answer our main questions, in particular about the reliability of Acts and Paul's relationship with Jesus.

But although we will not take the story much further, we will make a few brief comments on evidence from the later parts of Acts and of Paul's letters which is relevant to our questions.

The ongoing story in Acts

According to Acts Paul went on from Ephesus to Macedonia (20.1), and then travelled on to Achaia (i.e. probably to Corinth), where he stayed three months.

This is confirmed by 2 Corinthians and by Romans, a letter probably written from Corinth before Paul set off for Jerusalem and Rome (Romans 15.23–5, 16.1). 2 Corinthians fills out the picture of Acts in various ways, referring to a 'painful' visit made by Paul to Corinth (2.1), which Acts does not record, and describing some tensions between Paul and the Corinthians about his travel plans (1.15–24).

When Paul's stay in Corinth came to an end, he retraced his steps through Macedonia, then across the Aegean Sea to Troas and down the coast of the province of Asia (the west coast of Turkey) to Miletus, where he met with the elders of the Ephesus church at Miletus, and said his farewells to them. Paul then travelled on, eventually landing at Caesarea, and heading up to Jerusalem (Acts 20–1).

In Acts Paul's journey seems a little like Jesus' last journey to Jerusalem. He and others knew that sufferings awaited him in Jerusalem, and he speaks of not seeing those whom he meets again (20.22–3, 38, 21.4, 10–14). The writer of Acts may well have seen significance in the parallel between Jesus and Paul, but this does not mean that he invented the story. Paul's letter to the Romans tells against this, since Paul, writing from Corinth before setting out on the journey

1. speaks of his intention to go to Jerusalem (11.25);
2. makes it clear that he is intending to move on from his old mission fields to new regions in the West (15.19, 24). He has been operating from the church in Syrian Antioch, but now he is hoping to go to Spain, perhaps with Rome as his base (which is probably one of his reasons for writing to the Romans);
3. expresses his anxieties about dangers ahead in Jerusalem. He asks the Romans to pray 'that I may be rescued from the unbelievers in Judaea and that my service in Jerusalem may be acceptable to the saints there' (15.31). He knows, quite clearly, that he will be in danger from the Jews, for whom he is such a hated figure, but also that the Jewish Christians of Jerusalem have doubts about him, and that the financial gift that he is bringing might even be rejected. Paul wishes the gift to be an act of practical fellowship, but he is not sure that it will be received as such.

Given these points, the Acts picture of Paul's journey having a sense of foreboding and finality about it makes perfect sense.

It is interesting that, when he did arrive in Jerusalem, according to Acts both of Paul's fears as described in Romans were realized, at least to an extent. The Jewish Christians received Paul and his companions warmly, but expressed their anxiety about Paul's reputation as someone who 'teaches all the Jews who live among the Gentiles to turn away from Moses, telling them not to circumcise their children or live according to our customs' (21.22). As for the Jews, Acts says that some of the Jews from the province of Asia saw Paul in the temple, and stirred up a riot against him, accusing him of bringing unclean Greeks into the temple. Acts explains that they had seen a fellow Asian, Trophimus from Ephesus, with Paul in the city; earlier Acts had listed a whole group of people from different churches who accompanied Paul on all or part of his journey (20.4). The upshot of the riot was Paul's arrest, and then after various trials and a lengthy period of imprisonment in Caesarea he was transported to Rome for trial before Caesar, to whom he had appealed. Acts recounts Paul's journey to Rome, including a dramatic shipwreck story, and ends with Paul under house arrest and awaiting trial in Rome.

A considerable part of the concluding section of Acts is written in the first person (e.g. Acts 16.10a: 'After Paul had seen the vision, we got ready at once to leave'), and there is good reason to believe that it is a historical account: details such as the names of the Roman governors, Felix and Festus, are correct; the characterization of Felix as a corrupt man looking for a bribe (24.26–7) fits with the picture of him presented by the Roman historian Tacitus and others (Tacitus, *Annals* 12.54); and the shipwreck story shows every sign of being a first-hand account, well informed about places, weather conditions and maritime practices.

This last part of Paul's story in Acts is not very directly confirmed by his letters, though 2 Corinthians confirms that Paul took with him representatives of the churches that contributed to his collection (8.19–20). This is an interesting agreement with Acts, since Acts does not explain why Paul went up to Jerusalem with a lot of companions from different places, but 2 Corinthians makes clear that it was related to the collection, a measure designed to avert any criticism about the mishandling of funds. We can imagine how Paul's opponents would have liked to accuse him of embezzling money for his own purposes!

Various of Paul's letters confirm that he was in prison (Philippians 1.13; Colossians 4.10, 18; Philemon 1; 2 Timothy 1.8), but it is not certain where he was imprisoned, whether in Rome (as has traditionally been supposed), in Caesarea, or somewhere else. But the picture given in Acts of Paul being imprisoned for lengthy periods and in relatively civilized conditions fits well with the evidence of these letters. Of course, if the traditional view of the 'prison epistles' as written from Rome is correct, then they relate to a period of Paul's life that is not described in Acts, or scarcely so. In that case the failure of the letters to confirm the Acts story proves nothing at all.

Paul and Jesus in the later letters

In earlier chapters we have tried to work out from Paul's letters some of what he taught the churches that he founded, and in particular what he taught them about Jesus. We have noticed various clues about this, some strong, others more uncertain, and we have occasionally brought in the evidence of the later letters of Paul. We cannot go into detail about this and other evidence here, but we will note some of the possible allusions to the story and sayings of Jesus in the later letters.

In 2 Corinthians there are possible allusions to Jesus' characteristic way of introducing important sayings with the Hebrew word 'Amen' (= 'truly': 1.19–20), to his baptism as an anointing in which Christians share (1.22), to his transfiguration (3.18, 4.6), to his poverty and to his meekness and gentleness (8.9, 10.1), to apostles and miracles (12.12), and perhaps to his teaching about oaths (1.17).

In Romans the opening verses themselves are particularly intriguing, since Paul here describes his gospel or good news. We looked at such a description in 1 Corinthians 15.1–4, where the focus was exclusively on Jesus' death and resurrection, since Paul there is addressing the question of the resurrection of the dead. But in Romans 1.2–4 we have a broader summary of the gospel, which

- starts with God's promise through 'the prophets in the Holy Scriptures';
- focuses on
   God's Son,
   born as a descendant of David and
   finally rising powerfully from the dead.
   Jesus Christ our Lord;
- ends with a comment about apostles being sent with the good news to 'all the nations'.

There are lots of interesting things about this summary:

1. it has the story of Jesus at its heart, and not just the story of his death and resurrection, but the story from his birth to his resurrection;
2. there is a possible allusion to Jesus' virgin birth (the word 'born' being the verb 'become', as we saw when looking at Galatians 4.4);
3. Paul's summary here has a similar shape to a gospel like Matthew, which

- starts with a genealogy linking Jesus back to the Old Testament and Abraham,
- then tells the story of Jesus, 'Son of God' from his birth to his resurrection,
- ends with Jesus sending out the apostles to 'all the nations'.

This intriguing parallelism may be coincidental, but it may be that Paul's 'gospel' was much more like one of our written gospels than scholars have often supposed. The 'good news of Jesus Christ the Son of God' for Mark was the story of Jesus (Mark 1.1, 14.9); when Paul proclaimed the 'good news', was it a more abstract explanation of theological truths, or was it the story of Jesus, which he too saw as God's power for salvation?

Elsewhere in Romans:

- Jesus is portrayed as a second Adam (5.12–21), which, as we saw, might possibly be connected with Jesus' 'Son of Man' teaching;
- Paul refers to being baptized into the death of Christ (6.2–3), which may connect with Jesus' teaching about taking up the cross (e.g. Mark 8.34);
- Paul speaks of God 'sending out his Son' (8.3), which some have seen as an echo of Jesus' parable of the vineyard, where the distraught master sends his son to collect the fruit from the rebellious tenants (Mark 12.1–12);
- Paul refers to Christians crying 'Abba' through the Holy Spirit (8.15), reflecting Jesus' distinctive way of addressing God (cf. Mark 14.36);
- the sayings about blessing, not cursing enemies (12.14–21) resemble the Sermon on the Mount (Matthew 5.43–7; Luke 6.27–31);
- the instructions about paying taxes to the governing authorities (13.1–7) are reminiscent of Jesus' saying about 'paying Caesar what is Caesar's' (Mark 12.13–17; Matthew 22.15–22; Luke 20.20–6);
- the emphasis on love, which is the fulfilment of the law (12.9–10; 13.9–10), is similar to Jesus' teaching in Mark 12.28–34; Matthew 22.34–40;
- the encouragement to keep awake for the Lord's coming

(13.11–14) reminds us of Jesus' parables (and of the teaching of 1 Thessalonians);

- Paul encourages the strong not to cause the weak to stumble (chs. 14 and 15), and cites Jesus as the example (15.3); compare Jesus' teaching in Matthew 18.6–9 and elsewhere;
- Paul's reference to Christ being a servant of the Jews (15.7) is an interesting possible allusion to Jesus' comment on his mission in Matthew 15.24.

In Philippians the most interesting evidence is the 'Christ hymn', as it is sometimes called, in 2.5–11. Some people think that this 'hymn' antedates Philippians and has been appropriated by Paul. From our point of view, several things are interesting about it. First, it is in some ways very like Paul's summary of the gospel in Romans 1.3–4: the verses tell the story of Jesus, from his incarnation and birth to his death and resurrection, and end with reference to Jesus Christ as Lord and to him being worshipped in the whole world. The difference in Philippians is the focus on the humility of Christ, which is natural because the context in Philippians is a strong plea to live in unity and humility with each other (see 2.1–4). Second, the description of Jesus' humility as a slave, going even to death, closely resembles Jesus' teaching on servanthood in Mark 10.42–5 and also John 13, where Jesus' washing of the disciples' feet may be seen as an acted parable of his coming death. Third, the verb used of Jesus taking human likeness is the verb 'become' used in Galatians 4.4 and Romans 1.3, a word which may suggest that Paul knew of Jesus' virgin birth (see Chapter 7 above).

Philippians also speaks of Jesus' sufferings and resurrection (3.10), and about the coming of Christ, who 'will transform our lowly bodies to be like his glorious body' (3.21), a verse we noted in connection with 1 Corinthians 15.

Paul's later letters – Colossians, Ephesians, Philemon, 1 and 2 Timothy and Titus – are often regarded by scholars as 'pseudonymous', i.e. written in the name of Paul but not by Paul. We considered this possibility in connection with 2 Thessalonians, and saw good reason to doubt it in that case. Whether or not these other letters are by Paul, they also contain a variety of possible echoes of the story of Jesus.

Thus Colossians may echo Jesus' parables about seed and sowers (1.5); it has the interesting reference to 'the writing that stood against us [. . .] being nailed to the cross' (2.14), possibly an allusion to the accusation pinned to Jesus' cross by Pilate's soldiers (Matthew 27.37; Mark 15.26; Luke 23.38; John 19.19–21), and it refers to Christ as the 'master' of Christians who will reward and punish, recalling Jesus' parables about servants and masters (3.22—4.1). Its comment about conversation being seasoned with salt (4.6) reminds us of Jesus' words about Christians being called to be like salt (Matthew 5.13; Mark 9.50; Luke 14.34–5).

Ephesians speaks of the Church as a building whose cornerstone is Christ and as a holy temple where the Spirit dwells (2.20), themes which may perhaps be connected with the saying of Jesus about 'the stone which the builders rejected being the head of the corner' (Mark 12.10). Ephesians also quotes the Genesis text about husband and wife being one flesh (Ephesians 5.25–33), which Jesus cites when discussing marriage and divorce (Mark 10.1–12) and which Paul quotes in 1 Corinthians (6.16, 7.4). Ephesians also speaks of the need to stand and to pray in the day of evil (6.10–20), instructions which remind us of Jesus' exhortation to the disciples to keep awake and to 'pray [. . .] that you may be able to stand' (Luke 21.36).

In the so-called Pastoral Epistles which Paul addresses to his colleagues Timothy and Titus, there are various interesting references – to Christ as a ransom (1 Timothy 2.5; Titus 2.14; cp. Mark 10.45), to the 'labourer deserving his wages' (1 Timothy 5.17, referred to as a quote from 'the Scriptures'; cp. Luke 10.7), to the importance of the rich laying up treasure for eternal life (1 Timothy 5.19; cp. Jesus' sayings about laying up treasure in heaven in Matthew 6.19–20/Luke 12.33–4), and to sufferings in the last days and to persecution (2 Timothy 3.1–12; cp. Mark 13.5–13 etc.).

This is not an exhaustive list, and some of the clues are stronger evidence for Paul's familiarity with Jesus' teaching than others. But what is clear in any case is that the argument developed in the earlier chapters could have been extended by reference to the Pauline letters which we have not studied. It may be that some of the later letters have less obvious echoes of Jesus' teaching than some of the earlier letters. This could be taken to support those who question their authenticity (which would leave our argument about the importance of Jesus for Paul intact or even strengthened). But it is just as likely to be accidental, since we have seen that Paul's use of the sayings and stories of Jesus is a reflection of the particular issues of particular churches. It could also be that the misunderstandings and debates about Jesus' teaching were greatest in the earlier period, when Christians were thinking through so many issues for the first time, rather than in the later period, when the interpretation of Jesus' teaching will have become standardized and universal.

16 The true story

We have journeyed far enough with Paul to answer some of the questions with which we started this book. In particular we have been interested in knowing whether Paul was a rogue apostle (as some thought in the early Church, and some think today), claiming to follow Jesus but propounding a different gospel from that of Jesus. We have also been interested in whether the account of Paul's life and ministry in Acts is a trustworthy account, or a sanitized semi-fictional account. We have addressed these questions by travelling a long way with Paul: we have compared Acts and Paul's letters and tried to see how they relate to each other and to a wider historical context, and we have looked at the letters to see what they tell us about Paul and his ministry and in particular to see what light they shed on the question of Paul's knowledge of Jesus.

The story of Paul in Acts

Our examination of Acts has strongly confirmed its historical reliability. We have seen how various scholarly theories that cast doubt on Acts – for example, the widely held view that the Council of Acts 15 corresponds to the meeting of Paul with the Jerusalem leaders described in Galatians 2 – are actually thoroughly implausible. A thoughtful reading of Acts in the light of the historical context (including events such as the expulsion of the Jews from Rome) makes it clear that Acts gets the history right again and again.

Not that Acts tells us the whole story; how could it? There are things that were very important to Paul at particular times, such as the dispute with Peter in Antioch and the collection for Jerusalem, which were not important issues for the author of Acts at the time he wrote his narrative. But this is not a sinister whitewashing or romanticizing of history: why should Acts tell us all the details of the sharp dispute and debate in Antioch, highlighting Peter and Paul's temporary disagreement, which was quite quickly sorted out?

179

Why should Acts say much about the collection – though it is mentioned in 24.17 – when other things came to dominate Paul's final visit to Jerusalem, namely his arrest and trials?

The fact is that the evidence of Acts and of Paul's letters is strikingly complementary. The differences between them are important, showing that we have the testimony of different witnesses; the way they converge and throw light on each other's evidence suggests that we are dealing with reliable witnesses, whose testimony can be trusted. For example, Paul's references in 1 Thessalonians 2 to the sufferings of the Thessalonians and to the 'wrath' coming on the Jews fit like a glove with the evidence of Acts about Paul having to leave Thessalonica because of Jewish opposition and about his coming to Corinth, where he wrote 1 Thessalonians, just after the expulsion of the Jews from Rome and just after the terrible events that happened in Jerusalem at that time.

Acts, as we have said, appears to have been written by a companion of Paul. This is the natural inference from the use of the first person plural in the second half of Acts, starting with 16.10: 'After Paul had seen the vision, we got ready at once to leave for Macedonia.' Modern scholars have questioned whether these 'we' passages do necessarily show that the author of Acts was a companion of Paul, some proposing that the author may have used someone else's diary, others that it is a literary device. But neither of these suggestions is at all plausible. Even if a diary existed, the author of Acts was quite capable of incorporating it properly into his work, not leaving remnants of 'we' and giving the false impression that he was there. The idea of a deliberate literary device hardly washes, given how unselfconscious and intermittent the 'wes' seem to be. These suggestions only carry any weight because scholars have concluded on other grounds (such as the supposed discrepancies between Acts and Paul) that Acts is not reliable. However, given the evidence for the reliability of Acts we have examined, the obvious explanation of the 'we' passages is that the author was present.

The very early tradition of the Church is that Acts was written by Luke, the doctor who was one of Paul's companions, and that tradition is entirely credible. In any case, if Acts was by a companion of Paul, then in Acts and Paul's letters we have two independent eyewitness accounts of the events we have been discussing. The two accounts, as we have seen, fit together very well indeed.

The story of Jesus in Paul

But what of Paul and the story of Jesus? Paul has often been accused by scholars of doing his own thing, of changing the gospel of Jesus into something more like a Greek mystery religion, and of having little interest in the teaching of Jesus. The lack of direct references to Jesus' life and teaching in Paul's letters has been a major plank in this argument.

But we have seen that the argument is again resoundingly wrong! There is a huge amount of evidence that Paul's gospel included, at its core, stories and sayings of Jesus. And, although he doesn't often quote them directly in his letters, he indirectly refers and alludes to them frequently.

We have concentrated in this book on four of Paul's letters – Galatians, 1 and 2 Thessalonians, and 1 Corinthians. We argued that these are Paul's earliest extant letters. In them we have found evidence that Paul taught people about the death and resurrection of Jesus: he told them the story of the Last Supper, of the arrest of Jesus, of his crucifixion, his burial, and his resurrection, including the appearances of the risen Lord. We have found unmistakable evidence of Paul's familiarity with Jesus' teaching on the Second Coming, on ethical issues, such as divorce, and on ministry issues, such as apostleship. We have have found unmistakable evidence that he and his churches knew about Jesus addressing God as Abba, and saw this word of Jesus as something important.

In addition to this considerable amount of unmistakable evidence, there is also much other very plausible evidence which suggests that the stories and teaching of Jesus were important in Paul's churches, whether it was Jesus' command to love one another and to be servants to one another, his teaching about the kingdom of God, his teaching about cleanness and uncleanness, about Peter's primacy, about the temple, or about the priority of the Jews. Many of these issues seem to have been the subject of debate between Paul and his followers, the Corinthians using Jesus' teaching to advocate promiscuity on the one hand and celibacy on the other!

Some of the evidence is less strong. For example there are possible clues that Paul knew the stories of Jesus' birth, of his baptism, of his transfiguration. A wise detective would not build too much on this evidence by itself, but would look for other, less ambiguous evidence to corroborate or disprove his or her suspicions about its significance. In this case there is, as we have seen, a mass of less ambiguous evidence, and so what seemed possible but uncertain looks after all rather likely. In other words there is a significant cumulative argument for Paul knowing and teaching about Jesus' birth, baptism and transfiguration, to name just a few of the things we looked at.

The picture that emerges is that Paul probably knew much of what we know of Jesus from the gospels. There are things that do not come up in his letters; for example, Jesus' miracles get no direct mention, though even on this matter there is an indirect hint or two. This is not surprising, since, as we have seen, the things that come up in the letters are determined by the issues affecting the church to which Paul is writing.

What is impressive is how traditions of Jesus seem to be important on just about every topic that Paul discusses in his letters: whether it is the question of Paul's own apostleship in Galatia, the fate of Christians who have died in Thessalonica, or sex and marriage in Corinth, Paul draws deeply on traditions of Jesus in what he says. The story and sayings of Jesus were foundational for him and central to his teaching.

So much may be concluded quite securely. Rather more speculatively, we may wonder whether the way that scholars distinguish the word 'gospel' as used of Paul's preaching and the word as used of the written gospels is misleading. What was the good news that Paul preached? We have seen a number of clues which suggest that it was, or at least included, the story of Jesus. Thus in 1 Corinthians 15.1 he refers to the gospel he taught them, and proceeds to refer to Jesus' death, burial and resurrection. In that context, because he is going on to talk about resurrection, he starts the story with Jesus' death. But in Galatians 4.4 we perhaps have the opposite end of the story, when Paul says: 'When the time had fully come, God sent his Son, born of a woman, born under the law'. Romans 1.3–4 arguably brings them together: Paul here refers to 'the gospel', of which he is an apostle, and speaks of Jesus from his birth as a descendant of David to his resurrection from the dead; a similar pattern may be reflected in Philippians 2.5–11. In all these instances Paul is only summarizing and hinting at the full story, but it is at least possible that Paul's churches learned the 'good news' of Jesus in a form not dissimilar to our written gospels. That is not to suggest that, when Paul first arrived in a place, he stood up and (in effect) recited one of the gospels from end to end. Neither common sense nor the book of Acts suggests that. But it seems likely that Paul's evangelistic preaching will have included substantial explanation of Jesus' life and teaching, not just a few credal statements about his death and resurrection. It also seems quite possible that Paul's evangelistic missions will have included a systematic explanation of the story of Jesus – from his birth to his resurrection.

That conclusion is all the more likely if the author of Luke's gospel was a companion of Paul, as we have argued. The evidence is that Paul's missionary team included the gospel writer; if it did, then we may conclude that the story of Jesus was of interest and importance within Paul's team. In theory it could be that only Luke was interested, and that others, including Paul, were not. But, although it is conceivable that someone like Luke (and perhaps Mark before him) had a particular role as narrator of the Jesus story, it is most unlikely that this was an interest not shared by others. It is certainly not what Luke suggests in the book of Acts; he ends his account of Paul with the comment that 'Boldly and without hindrance he preached the kingdom of God and taught about the Lord Jesus Christ' (Acts 28.31). It is also not what our study of Paul has suggested, since we have seen ample evidence that Paul was interested in Jesus. It is not unreasonable to deduce that Luke's gospel gives us a good idea of what Paul's churches would have been taught about Jesus.

This fits in with what we have noticed in the course of our study about Paul having various things in common with Luke. For example, in Galatians we saw how Paul's description of Jesus being born of a woman under the law sounded like Luke's infancy narrative; in 1 Thessalonians we saw how Paul's references to 'the wrath' and to the suddenness of the Lord's coming sound like words of Jesus in Luke 21; in 1 Corinthians we noticed how Jesus' words at the Last Supper are the same in Luke and 1 Corinthians, and how the Corinthians may well have known the Lukan story of Mary and Martha and the Lukan version of Jesus' saying about resurrection life.

On the other hand, we have also found that Paul knows things that are in the other gospels, including the commissioning of Peter in Matthew 16.16–20, the sayings about mission being limited to the Jews, and the parable of the wise and foolish virgins. This evidence in no way undermines the overall argument; it simply suggests that Luke tells us a lot about the stories and sayings of Jesus known in Paul's churches, but not everything. Luke and indeed all of the evangelists have been selective, and Paul attests to things found in each of them, including John (the command to 'love one another').

If our preceding argument about Paul and Jesus is along the right lines, then those who say that Paul's 'silence' about Jesus' life shows his lack of serious interest in Jesus' earthly ministry are entirely mistaken. Paul in fact is not silent at all; the echoes of Jesus' teaching and the allusions to his life are everywhere. As for his failure to quote traditions of Jesus more explicitly or more often, this is well explained if, as the evidence suggests, the stories and sayings of Jesus had been passed on by Paul and his companions when they brought the good news to a place. His letters were follow-up documents, dealing with 'matters arising', and so he did not usually need to repeat the well-known traditions. On the other hand, he could and did allude to them, expecting his hearers to pick up the allusions. For Paul the sound foundation of God's church was not just an abstract theological concept of Jesus, but Jesus' life and teaching, his death and resurrection, his present Lordship and his coming again.

The true stories of Paul and Jesus

Introducing Paul

We concluded that Acts tells us a true story of Paul. And when we put Acts and Paul's letters together, the picture we find of Paul is impressive, one of a man captured by the grace of God and reflecting that grace in tireless ministry to others. It is helpful to put Paul's letters in the context of the story of Acts, not just because this illuminates some tricky issues, but also because we will be reminded that the letters come from an active, strenuous, committed ministry, not from a comfortable theologian's study isolated from reality. It is helpful to read Paul's letters along with Acts, because the letters not only tell us a lot about the churches that he founded – 1 Corinthians gives us an unparalleled picture – but because they reveal much of the passion and pain that characterized Paul's ministry. Some people imagine that Paul was a difficult person to get on with, and clearly he did fall out with Peter at least once, and twice with that wonderful man Barnabas, who did so much for him. But he was reconciled to both and, even if his strong convictions made him uncompromising on some things, on other things he is intensely human and caring. He agrees with the views of the 'stronger' on food offered to idols, but firmly disagrees with their insistence on their own views at the expense of the 'weaker'. He disagrees with the super-spiritual who think that sex and the body are fleshly and should be suppressed by Christians; he inspires love and respect in colleagues and converts, and cares very deeply about them; he has the reputation for being stronger in his letters and weaker in person (2 Corinthians 10.10). I suspect that many people will be surprised how gentle and loving this author of 1 Corinthians 13 is, when they meet him in heaven!

As for the doubts that some people have about Paul's faithfulness to Jesus, there are obvious differences, at least superficially, between Jesus' kingdom teaching and Paul's teaching about justification and about being 'in Christ'. But we have shown that Paul was very interested in the teaching and story of Jesus, seeking to model his life and ministry on the one he saw as Lord. And we have seen numerous points of continuity between Jesus' message and Paul's teaching (something that I explore in detail in my earlier *Paul, Follower of Jesus or Founder of Christianity?*). Not that Paul made no original contribution of his own to the development of Christianity. On the contrary, he made a vital contribution in working out, with his churches, what it meant to follow Jesus in a Gentile world *after* Jesus' death and resurrection (such hugely important events), *after* Pentecost and the gift of the Spirit, and *before* his return. But, although his new context inevitably meant that Paul had to address new issues which Jesus had not discussed, the evidence we have examined shows that Jesus remained foundational for him. The message of Jesus (or 'the word of Christ': Colossians 3.16) and the example of Jesus (1 Corinthians 11.1) and above all the death and resurrection of Jesus were at the heart of his ministry.

It is also worth noting that, when we observe Paul dealing with difficult issues, for example the issue of spiritual gifts and of sexuality in Corinth, his handling of them is balanced and impressive: he affirms the miraculous spiritual gifts, but insists on the priority of the love of God and the way of the cross. This is surely a faithful interpretation of Jesus, who worked miracles, but then set his face to the cross. Paul affirms freedom in Christ through the Spirit and the equality of the sexes in Christ, but affirms also the goodness of creation, of the body and of the differences between men and women, thus ruling out both the immorality and the unisex asceticism of different members of the Corinthian church. Again Paul's interpretation of Jesus seems unerringly sound. The idea that Paul was a misogynist and an ascetic spoilsport, who subverted the positive teachings of Jesus, misses the mark totally; the contrary is the case. When Paul says that 'we have the mind of Christ', he is speaking of Christians generally, not exclusively of himself (1 Corinthians 2.16), but it is a sentiment that we may see as conspicuously true of him, as an intelligent, caring, flexible and faithful interpreter of Jesus.

The question of Jesus

This book has focused on Paul, but in view of what we have said about Paul and Jesus, it may not be out of place to end with a comment about Jesus, since our study has some interesting implications for the question of the truth of the story of Jesus.

For Christian faith there is probably no more important question than whether the gospel stories of Jesus are true. All sorts of doubts have been raised about them, all sorts of theories put forward to explain the gospels, and in particular their relationship to one other. Scholars mostly agree that the gospels were all written sometime in the first century, but on other matters there are wide differences of opinion.

We cannot explore these often very complicated questions in this book. But our study is relevant to them for three reasons. First, it shows how important the stories and sayings of Jesus were during Paul's mission and when he was writing his letters, in other words within a decade or two of Jesus' own lifetime. Scholars tend to date the gospels around AD 60 or later, and some suppose that the stories and sayings of Jesus were rather inaccurately remembered in the years before they were written down. Granted, a lot can be forgotten in thirty years. But Paul's evidence shows that Christians were carefully teaching and learning about Jesus from the very earliest days of the Church onwards, while eyewitnesses (friendly and hostile!) were still alive.

Second and more specifically, if we are right in suspecting that Paul, writing in the late 40s AD, knew the stories of Jesus' birth (such as we find them in Luke), to take one example, or Jesus' parable of the wise and foolish virgins (recorded in Matthew), to take another, then this is important corroboration for those stories, and many others like them. Paul's evidence also throws light on questions to do with the different gospels. Scholars mostly think that Mark is the earliest gospel, and this may well be right. But Paul suggests that Mark is not our only trustworthy source of information; stories and sayings found only in Luke or Matthew (or even John) also go back very early indeed.

Third and finally, we have shown that Luke is a good and well-informed historian in his telling of Paul's story in Acts. If that is true of his second volume, then there must be every chance that it is true of his first volume about Jesus too.

Luke starts his gospel with an impressive claim to accuracy: 'Many have undertaken to draw up an account of the things that have been fulfilled among us, just as they were handed down to us by those who from the first were eyewitnesses and servants of the word. Therefore, since I myself have accurately investigated everything from the beginning, it seemed good also to me to write an orderly account for you, most excellent Theophilus, so that you may know the certainty [or 'safety'] of the things you have been taught' (Luke 1.1–4). This opening to the gospel, with its use of expressions such as 'accurately', 'eyewitness' and 'know the certainty', sounds like an author who wants his account to be seen as serious history. It could be a purely formal opening of no real significance for the question of historicity, and some scholars have taken it as such. But in view of what we have seen in looking at Acts, this scholarly opinion seems highly questionable.

Of course, there are no 'we' passages in Luke, and so he could be reliable in Acts and unreliable in the gospel. But the 'we' passages only start halfway through Acts, and we have found the earlier parts (e.g. to do with Paul's conversion) to be well founded. This author could do his research! Admittedly the gospel describes things prior to Paul (whose companion Luke was, if the author was Luke), but the author appears to have been in Palestine with Paul for a length of time (see the 'we' passages in Acts 21.27, 27.1, etc.), and it seems likely that the author who wrote Luke 1.1–4 would have done his research on Jesus as thoroughly as his research on later matters. If he has taken trouble to give us a trustworthy story of Paul, as we argued, then we may guess that he will have done the same with the story of Jesus.

These three strands of evidence on the question of Jesus are important. We have compared our task in this book to that of a detective, trying not to jump to conclusions prematurely, but piecing together different items of evidence and seeing how they fit together. What we have found is a fascinating web of converging evidence – from Acts, from Paul's letters and from the gospels, not to mention Josephus and other ancient historians. What does this evidence suggest with regard to the question: is the New Testament story of Jesus 'true'? We might spend a long time defining exactly what we mean by the word 'true'. But if what we are asking is whether the New Testament story of Jesus is based on good history, then the answer towards which our evidence points is yes.

The evidence we have examined in this book points to us having a true story of Paul and a true story of Jesus too.

Index of biblical references

189

Index of biblical references

Index of subjects

Abba 63–4, 66, 148, 175
Abomination of Desolation 103, 117
Abraham 30, 50, 52, 53–5, 56, 58, 175
Acts of the Apostles xi, 13, 22, 129, 179–81; *see also* Index of Biblical References
Adam (and Eve) 130, 133, 139, 150, 165–7, 175
Agabus 31, 34
Alexandria 121, 122
Amen 174
Ananias 19–20
Antioch (in Syria) 22, 26–36, 39, 40, 43, 44, 45, 46–7, 48, 79, 121
Antiochus IV Epiphanes 103, 116–17
Apollos 101, 121–2, 124, 136, 137, 140, 141, 158, 160
Apostle(ship) xi, 8, 10, 22, 23, 29, 50, 51, 68–72, 109, 112, 145, 146–7, 156–61, 162, 175
Aquila and Priscilla 82, 85, 87–90, 121, 122, 123, 124, 125
Arabia 22, 23, 24–5, 51
Aramaic 3, 7, 63–4, 71, 93, 107, 136, 165, 166
Aretas 24
Athens 81, 84, 86–7
Atonement, Day of 15, 56
Authenticity: of gospel traditions 186–8; of Pauline letters 112–15, 120, 176
Authority 156–60

Baptism 19, 53, 66–7, 73–4, 122, 124, 128, 130, 131, 137, 139, 141, 161–2, 174
Barnabas xi, 21, 28–9, 30–5, 39–44, 45, 46, 47, 51, 60, 77–9, 95, 121
Birth of Jesus 64–6, 174, 176
Body 128, 132, 139, 148–9

Caesar *see* Rome/Romans
Celibacy 131–4, 150–3; *see also* Marriage
Charismatic gifts *see* Gifts (spiritual)
Christ *see* Messiah
Circumcision 32, 41, 46, 50, 51, 73, 78
Claudius, emperor 90
Clean, unclean 11, 12, 27, 108, 134, 154
Collection for Jerusalem 30–1, 33–6, 125–6, 173

Colossae, Colossians 123–4; *see also* Index of Biblical References
Conversion of Paul xi, xii, 8, 9, 12, 13–18, 19, 20, 21, 22, 30, 55, 143, 147, 149
Corinth/Corinthians xii, 81–4, 86, 87, 121, 122, 124, 127–42, 143–68; *see also* Index of Biblical References
Cornelius 45
Council of Jerusalem 32, 35, 47–8, 77–9
Creation 130–1, 135, 138, 156, 166
Creation/new creation 9, 52
Curse 11, 52, 56
Cyprus 21, 27, 28, 39, 45, 77, 78

Damascus (Road) 9, 10, 13, 14, 15, 16, 17, 20, 22, 23, 24–5, 26, 55, 96, 147
Deacon 7
Death 93–4, 96, 98–9; of Jesus 10, 14–15, 18, 53, 56, 62, 73, 76, 143–9, 175, 177
Devil *see* Satan
Disciples 124, 149
Discipline (Church) 165
Divorce 5, 149–51, 154

Elders *see* Leaders, Church
End 104; *see also* Second coming
Ephesus/Ephesians 78, 121–6, 139, 141; *see also* Index of Biblical References
Eschatological discourse 96–7, 116, 117, 118, 120
Eschatology *see* Second coming
Ethics 50, 58, 108, 131–4
Eucharist *see* Lord's Supper
Evangelism 81–2, 85–7, 183
Expulsion of Jews from Rome 82–3, 87–90, 141

Faith 51, 53–5, 162
Father 63–4; *see also* Abba
Fellowship, participation 149
Flesh 58, 148, 150
Food 46–8, 132, 134–6, 138, 153–6
Forgiveness 67, 73
Foundation 160–1

Index of subjects

The Society for Promoting Christian Knowledge (SPCK) was
founded in 1698. Its mission statement is:

To promote Christian knowledge by

- **Communicating the Christian faith in its
  rich diversity**
- **Helping people to understand the Christian faith
  and to develop their personal faith; and**
- **Equipping Christians for mission and ministry**

SPCK Worldwide serves the Church through Christian
literature and communication projects in 100 countries, and
provides books for those training for ministry in many parts of
the developing world. This worldwide service depends upon the
generosity of others and all gifts are spent wholly on ministry
programmes, without deductions.

SPCK Bookshops support the life of the Christian community
by making available a full range of Christian literature and other
resources, providing support for those training for ministry, and
assisting bookstalls and book agents throughout the UK.

SPCK Publishing produces Christian books and resources,
covering a wide range of inspirational, pastoral, practical and
academic subjects. Authors are drawn from many different
Christian traditions, and publications aim to meet the needs of a
wide variety of readers in the UK and throughout the world.

The Society does not necessarily endorse the individual views
contained in its publications, but hopes they stimulate readers to
think about and further develop their Christian faith.

For information about the Society, visit our website at
www.spck.org.uk, or write to:
SPCK, Holy Trinity Church, Marylebone Road,
London NW1 4DU, United Kingdom.